The Way Out

by Jennifer Schulman

Edited by Aaron Schulman

ISBN: 978-1-7353429-1-7 (paperback)

All emphases in Scripture quotations are the author's.

Disclaimer
The Way Out recounts one woman's experiences with trauma, faith, and healing. It is not a substitute for medical or psychological treatment. Readers experiencing emotional distress should seek help from qualified professionals. Advice given is based on the author's personal journey and spiritual insights; individual results may vary.

Edited by Aaron Schulman
Jennifer Schulman's manuscript was meticulously edited and refined by Aaron Schulman, bringing clarity and coherence to her powerful story through every stage of the editorial process.

First Edition – June 2025

Publisher
Self-published by Jennifer Schulman
c/o Aaron Schulman, Editor
www.WayOutBook.com

Printed in the United States of America.

JOIN US & BECOME A VIP

You're not alone… and your journey is just beginning.

You picked up "The Way Out" for a reason.
Maybe you're confronting deep wounds.
Maybe you're supporting someone you love.
Maybe you're simply hoping someone understands.

We do. And we're offering to walk with you…

Take the Next Step — Walk Deeper with Us

Introducing the "Way Out AudioBook & Intimate Conversations"
More than just audio... it's healing, raw, and real.

Jennifer reads each chapter aloud, then she and Aaron share unfiltered, heart-level conversations about every topic - offering insights from 21+ years of healing in marriage, trauma recovery, and life with Jesus.

Real Stories. Real Healing. Real Breakthrough.
* Listen while driving, walking, or with your small group
* Perfect for journaling or deep discussions
* Hours of honest, Spirit-led audio you'll return to for life

FREE VIP ACCESS - Just for Readers - Get exclusive content when you join:
* FREE sample of our Audio + Conversation Series
* First access to new workshops & livestreams
* VIP-only videos, teachings & healing tools
* Bonus activations & behind-the-scenes insights

SCAN THIS QR CODE NOW - to unlock your free material and one-time offer - Only available to readers like you or visit: www.wayoutbook.com/VIP

Your journey toward healing doesn't end with a book. It begins with a relationship - With God… with yourself… and with a community that's walked the road too… We'll walk it with you.

— Jennifer & Aaron Schulman

Dedication

There is no way that I'd be the woman that I am today if it were not for the love of my life. Aaron, you woke my heart up. You have shown me what true love is. I love you more than words can express and I dedicate this book, our story, to you. You are my best friend and have shown me Jesus more than anyone that I've ever known.

To my oldest daughter, my darling Rachel. I have loved you from the moment that I knew about you. I can't imagine what it must have been like for you to watch your mommy fall apart in order to be put back together again. You were so brave. It all started with your prophetic word over me. You said that God will tear down this temple but will rebuild it again. I am amazed at the woman that you've become and I am so proud of you! I pray that you embrace all that God has for you!

To my darling daughter, Linda. Your child-likeness and playfulness has freed me more than I thought possible. I am so proud of who you are becoming and treasure your heart more than life itself! You encourage me every single day to be myself and live like a little child. I love you!

To my precious daughter, Joy. You exude Joy and my heart is so full every time I watch you just jump. Before you were born, I received an email from a friend who, while praying for me, saw you. You were jumping up and down for joy. We named you Anointed Joy! You live that out every single day. You encourage me by the authentic, childlike way that you live and it has healed my soul in more ways than I ever thought possible. I love you! I am proud of you!

Years ago when everyone else left, Jim Davis stayed. Our church abandoned us because of how messy things had become in our life. Our Pastor actually told me that he wished that I'd hurry up and get over my past so that he could just "hang out" with Aaron. Another Pastor told me that "this church isn't for everyone". Jim walked right into our lives, rolled up his sleeves and his britches and stayed. He listened through the hard stuff. He looked me right in the eye and said, I'm staying . . I'm not going anywhere and I will be your dad. That man kept his word and I will never forget him. Jim's presence was exactly what I needed during this season of my life. He is a big part of my story and you will read more about him in this book. Jim - I love you. Thanks for being my dad when I needed you to be exactly that!

Bert Robinson - a dad, a grandfather, a friend. Thank you for being all of those things in different seasons of our life. You have held us to the fire and loved us well. I can't think of a time when we needed you and you weren't there. You have shown us courage and the value of a true friend. You are a great man and we love you and will always treasure you!

I want to name everyone but I know that I can't. All through my life I have encountered women and men who have loved me, encouraged me and sharpened me. I really need to thank my friend Diane Harper. She saw me at the very beginning of my healing journey and drew me right into her life. She loved me and accepted me just the way I was back then. What a wonderful mother she has been and exactly what I needed during that season of life!

I thank my God every day for Dawn. I have known this woman for more than half of my life. Dawn prayed and loved me right into the Kingdom! This book would not be possible without her friendship and loyalty!

I thank God every day for Marion Jos, Kathleen Sattler, Sharon Thompson for your unconditional love and acceptance of me. Your love and friendship has softened my heart and given me fuel to love others. I love each of you so much and thank God for you every day!

I am forever grateful for Erica Foster for being one of my greatest encouragers and for cheering me on with this book, this message. You carry such a beautiful humility that really inspires me and draws me to our Humble King. I value your testimony and you, your family . . are my family.

I am grateful for every man and every woman who has loved me, prayed for me and encouraged me in my life. I love you!

Last but not least, I am thankful for each person, who, while professing a love for Jesus, also abandoned my family during the darkest season of my life. It has shown me how to really pray for those in the church who do not really know what love is and haven't really learned about the sufferings of Christ and have not learned the meaning of true friendship. God used that experience to soften my heart for others who have also been abandoned. My heart has become stout yet not bitter. I have learned how to be a friend and I have gained courage that I never thought possible. Mostly, I am thankful for your absence because it made room for true friends that I will treasure throughout all of eternity. My prayer for you is that you will be given another chance but will be ready for it. There is nothing greater than walking through dark parts of people's lives and then getting to see the gold on the other side.

Table of Contents

by Section & Chapter

SECTION THREE: Transformation & Identity

After the digging comes the becoming. Here, you'll begin to rediscover who you are beyond abuse, rejection, and fear. These chapters help you rebuild your voice, your trust, and your God-given identity—piece by piece.

SECTION FOUR: Redemption & Restoration

This is the rising. The chapters here carry the sound of resurrection—joy after mourning, fruit from ashes, and bold declarations of hope. You'll see how God not only heals, but redeems. Not only restores, but multiplies. This is what it looks like when love has the final word.

Foreword

I don't know of anyone more brave than Jennifer.

She's overcome more than any human being I know. What you are holding in your hand is not just a book with a beautiful cover and clear, unique, catchy title, but an actual roadmap to life, freedom, and abundance - the way God intended for us.

This journey, once thought impossible, has become a roadmap of freedom, a highway of hope, and truly the way out of bondage from deep abuse and trauma into a fulfilling and empowered life. And this book was written by the bravest person I know - and I can say that because, for over 20 years, I have watched her live it out loud.

It's not just a book; it's a treasure map to freedom.

Not only has she come through the darkest of trauma, abuse, and betrayal, she has come out as a champion and torch bearer who has been living the last several years of her life fighting for the freedom of others - her family being first.

Anyone who has met Jennifer and has been brave enough to join and stay with her at "the table," as she has called it for years, has grown to a deeper place of love, trust, relationship, freedom, and life.

Others who have either remained in hiding, the shadows of performance, or outright remained opposed to staying at the table with Jennifer have missed one of life's greatest opportunities. For the faint of heart - and for those who prefer the safety of masks, inauthenticity, and performance - it will be nearly impossible to stay in a relationship with Jennifer for very long. She refuses to hide or return to the prison cell that Jesus freed her from.

She desires the same for every person who encounters her. Her loving yet no-nonsense approach to life and relationships is a challenging breath of fresh air for those who are truly brave hearts - and intimidating or threatening to both narcissists and those who are not ready to be truly free.

A walk with Jennifer is a challenging life that will accept nothing less than the full freedom that Jesus paid for - a life that many desire but are unwilling to traverse.

And in her life, what the enemy meant for evil, God has truly turned into good - for our family, and for so many others who have experienced the Jennifer that I am blessed to be married to. Yes, she is a challenge to me as well, but the blessing is in that challenge.

It's the mix of truth and love that she carries that sometimes cuts to the core - because she has truly broken free, and her freedom and authenticity are always a threat to those who are not ready, or who are comfortable living a hidden, lonely life. Because of her, I am a much better man and person, and can honestly say I would never have become the man that I am without having her as a gift in life - as my wife.

It wasn't always that way. The first few years of our marriage, we had no idea how it would ever work, as the wounds began to break open and the poison began to surface. ***But Jesus...***

We decided, day after day, we had only two choices: give up and remain in safe shackles like so many others do, or risk the sometimes terrifying decision to "let Him."

The effects that abuse has on human beings are more complex, dark, and debilitating than anything we have ever encountered. It's also one of the most difficult things to overcome - to the point where one is able to live a life of freedom, trust, and love toward others.

The difference isn't another counseling session, self-help book, medication, or support group - it's Jesus.

Many people we have encountered along the way—those who have been through similar trauma - are either still locked up behind fear and performance, coping the best they know how, or they are literally locked up in prison.

Jennifer bravely chose the higher way - not just once, but daily over the past 20-plus years. And those few who have allowed her to become close friends have experienced perhaps the most powerful, pure, honest, and truthful form of love and friendship a person could ever have.

Her freedom and the way she lives out loud for Jesus have brought many into a closer walk with God, a walk that exudes more freedom.

Jennifer learned one simple phrase - you could even consider it a prayer - early in her healing journey. The same simple phrase you will see throughout the book:

"Let Him."

When someone has been abused as a child and young adult, the idea of "let Him" is not only terrifying - it makes no sense. On the surface, it would seem like a deadly decision. Letting "Him" is a choice child abuse victims never had.

Yet the very same idea that is terrifying to an abuse victim is the one thing needed in order to find the way out of deep trauma and into abundant life - the life that Jesus paid for with His own brutal sacrifice.

Jennifer learned to embrace her simple prayer - one I believe she spoke to herself countless times in the dark - and now speaks to others as the true "way out."

Let Him.

This is my wife, Jennifer. I have seen her take rejection, betrayal, misunderstanding, and deep, unspeakable trauma and pain from her past, and courageously put one foot in front of the other - risking to surrender, trust, and love one more time, one more day, one day at a time. Love and trust can be unbearably painful at times, but it is the only way…

Her daily decision to "let Him" opened the "permission door," allowing Jesus to enter and do what only He can do. But it requires courage - and a daily decision to continue to say "yes" to the only One who has the resurrection power to heal and restore people to their right design, and to an abundantly blessed life, the way He originally intended.

Her life now embodies this truth in a way that many might not get to experience - that "with God, all things are possible!"

With God, Jennifer has not only overcome the deepest toxic personal trauma, but has grown into someone who now loves courageously and lights the path for others to boldly step into their freedom, one day at a time, by following her simple - yet sometimes terrifying - decision to simply "let Him."

Let Jennifer walk with you through the pages of this book - this treasure map - because along the way, if you stay courageous and continue to say yes, continue to "let Him," you will not only find a deeper, richer life with God, but you will gain the best friend anyone could imagine. And you will uncover - and learn to treasure - the value of what He created when He dreamed of you.

Let Him…

—

Aaron Schulman
(Jennifer's husband)

Introduction

Dear Beloved,

This book wasn't written from a desk - it was born from a battlefield.

Over the course of my life, I've walked through deep valleys: childhood trauma, domestic abuse, spiritual confusion, and years of silent suffering. I didn't always have language for the pain, let alone tools for healing. But Jesus did. And He was faithful to lead me, step by step, into freedom - not just emotionally, but spiritually, mentally, and relationally.

For more than two decades now, I've been on a journey of restoration. Not just for my sake, but for the sake of others - women, families, even churches—who need a safe and Spirit-led path toward wholeness.

The Way Out is more than a book - it's a roadmap, a strategy guide, and a treasure hunt. It's a conversation, a collection of insights, prayers, and Spirit-led activations designed to help you process, heal, and grow.

And it's not just for those who have experienced trauma or abuse. It's also for those who want to love, lead, or walk alongside someone who has. Whether you're on your own healing journey or supporting someone else's, these pages offer a path forward - full of grace, truth, and restoration.

My prayer is that as you read, you'll not only find language for your pain, but also hope for your restoration - and most of all, the tender nearness of a God who sees, knows, and heals.

This isn't just my story - it's yours too. May these pages be an invitation, a mirror, and a hand gently extended to say:

There is a way out. And you are not alone.

I wrote "The Way Out" as a companion for those walking through the hard, holy work of healing - especially from the kind of trauma that changes everything.

This is not a book you rush through. It's a road map to the way for hope and overcoming. And it's meant to be walked, every step, with Jesus.

Each chapter was born out of my own lived experiences - heartbreak, healing, marriage, grief, forgiveness, joy, and deep encounters with God. These are my stories, but I believe they'll speak to yours too.

Here's how to navigate through this book:

• Take your time. Some chapters will hit deep. When they do, pause. Pray. Journal. Sit with Jesus. You don't have to "finish" this book - you just have to be with it.

• Bring a notebook. There are no official "prompts," but don't be surprised if the Holy Spirit starts writing back to you in the margins.

• Start where you need to. While the chapters flow in a healing order, you can jump around. If you're in a moment of grief, go to "Joy Comes in the Mourning." If you're struggling with shame, start with "Don't Downplay Your Pain." Let the Spirit guide you.

• Make space for God. This isn't just a book of insight. It's an invitation - to rest, to wrestle, to be held, and to be known by a God who still heals.

My prayer is that The Way Out helps you feel seen, known, and gently led by Jesus out of the places that once held you captive. And when you're ready - you'll find the strength not just to walk out, but to lead others into freedom too.

You are so loved.
There is hope.
And there is always a way out.

With you on the journey,

—Jennifer

SECTION ONE: Foundations & First Cracks

Before healing can begin, we must name where we've come from. This section holds the roots - your history, your heartbreak, and the people and promises that shaped you. It's the starting point for your walk out of pain and into purpose.

Chapter 1

Jesus

The Alpha and Omega. How can I start this book without Jesus? I don't enter rooms without Him in front. I'm certainly not going to enter into this sacred space without my Best Friend!

While I distinctly remember meeting Him at 21, I believe I encountered Him earlier in my life. I see the Blood thread all through my life. That Blood is the only reason that I am here, writing this book and praying for you.

Sure, He saved my soul but His saving, loving work of redemption and refinement continues in my life. I will never forget my first head on collision with Jesus Christ. It was transformational and electric. It was BIG. I felt it in every part of my body and it was not only obvious to me but those around me. I lost a lot of friends and was mocked by my family. I had more zeal than I did knowledge and irritated a lot of "religious" people back then.

I look back at those years now and can very clearly see how I was radically transformed and dropped into a new life. Do you think that the enemy stopped trying to destroy me then? Nope. The battle just became intense. We'll get more into that later.

I give Jesus the credit, the glory, the praise, the dedication and all of my attention through this entire story. It belongs to us… Him and me. Without Jesus there is absolutely no way I would ever have been delivered and set free to be able to share with you - I wouldn't have a testimony.

He has been with me from the moment He thought of me (psalm 139) and will be with me throughout all of eternity. He will never leave me, never forsake me. I am His prize, His gem, His special girl, the apple of His eye and He loves me.

I can tell you this, dear one . . . . Jesus is with you in the darkest and most cringing hour of your life. He always has been. I know, I know . . . hard to accept that. Trust me! I know the trigger that may be right now for you. It was for me. I was so angry and hurt and betrayed.

If Jesus loved me so much, then why did He let me go through that? Why didn't He stop it? I know! That is a very good question and I promise you that He is not afraid of that question. I struggled with that for years, even after learning to love Him. One day, I ventured into that with Him.

When you are ready - you will also venture into that with Him. He will come boldly and He will show you. I want to ask you to be willing to receive what He shows you. Ok? Be brave. I'm so proud of you for daring to go there with me, with Jesus!

I love Him. He is the Man of my dreams and He takes me places that I never thought possible. He has made my dreams come true and there's more! I wake up everyday with an expectation of . . . the more. What's next?

His heart is like the heart of a child. So good and true and pure. His love is endless and unconditional and has no limits. I love Him. Oh, have you danced with Jesus yet?

I wanted to start this book with Him. I wanted for Him to start this book. I am giving Jesus Chapter 1. The Alpha.

If you have not met the Man of Fire - let me introduce you.

It's Jesus, Messiah, Son of God, Lion of Judah, Saviour of the world, Lamb of God. The One who laid down His life to heal you, save you, live with you, redeem, restore, be your breath, be your ALL! He loves you!

Behold, the Son of the Most High God! He is here. He sees, knows, loves, wants, hears YOU.

Repent and let Him love you!

Just ask . . .

Ask Him to show you who He is - He will.

Chapter 2

Me

I'm reclined in my big leather chair, soaking in His Presence, thinking about you. I'm struggling today. Today, I'm not terribly excited about living inside of my own skin. ***Do you ever feel that way?***

What I mean by that is, it seems like I've never been 100% comfortable with myself. I have struggled with deep insecurities all of my life. I live inside of my head most of the time. Sometimes I'm a bit analytical and therefore analyze every relationship and everything that was said or has been done. Maybe I'm just a perfectionist and when I feel like I've dropped the ball, I beat myself up for days. I'm me and no one else gets to do it. No one can love Jesus the way that I do. Sometimes, though, it's just hard.

As I get older and my relationship with Jesus gets deeper - the more uncomfortable I become in my skin. The closer I get to Him, the more aware I am of my weaknesses, my flaws, my poor habits. The more aware that I become of these fleshy things - the more frustrated I become.

To me, "fleshy things" are simply those feelings, burdens, and experiences that are challenging or awkward and sometimes debilitating simply because we are not at home yet, and have not stepped into the full promise yet of incorruptible bodies as we are promised at the resurrection in 1 Corinthians 15. We're still working out our salvation in a fallen world and like Paul said in Romans 7:24-25, "who will free me from this body of death?"

And then I saw it… there it is, in plain sight… ***the way out…***

"What an agonizing situation I am in! So who has the power to rescue this miserable (woman) man from the unwelcome intruder of sin and death? I give all my thanks to God, ***for his mighty power has finally provided <u>a way out</u> through our Lord Jesus***, the Anointed One! So if left to myself, the flesh is aligned with the law of sin, but now my renewed mind is fixed on and submitted to God's righteous principles." (Romans 7:24-25 TPT; emphasis & underline added)

I can remember when these emotions would cause me to go into hiding. I would be overwhelmed by these struggles and believe that these things were my identity. Then the shame would build and the guilt was unbearable. I would go into hiding.

Now? I run even harder towards Him.

I am moving along in years and I'm still searching to be grounded and to be more balanced. I don't have all of the answers. I have raised 1 daughter and am still raising 2 more. Aaron and I have been married for more than 2 decades and it's been work, sometimes very difficult work. If you think marriage is easy - don't get married.

I have been a believer since I was 21.

The day that I turned 16, my parents told me to just quit school and get a job. I did. I got a job and I worked hard. I was stuck.

I met a guy when I was freshly 17 and thought that he was my way out. I married him to get away from a toxic home life. He was a lunatic.

8 months into this so-called relationship.... he hit me for the very first time. He was an alcoholic and abused drugs. He was very mean. There was no one to save me now. I left an abusive life and went straight into another. I was completely hopeless. He had several women. Even brought them home occasionally for me to meet and be humiliated. I personally thought that he was the devil himself.

This went on for a few years. Every time I'd leave - he found me. The beatings got worse until one day, I knew, if I didn't leave, he'd kill me. I waited until he was gone and I knew I had a very small amount of time to get out. I did. I had to move out of the city and go into hiding. I was 20, maybe.

My friend Dawn... she had been praying for me... for a long time. She and I were close. I don't want to share any details about her because I didn't get her permission. She was my only friend for a long time. She invited me to church all of the time. I always declined . . . until one day. I went. I hated being there. We'll get into that later on in the book. I left early because I was just so uncomfortable.

She invited me again and I went. I was under so much conviction and I could feel the weight of His Glory and I couldn't resist any longer. I got up out of that seat and ran down front! I grabbed that preacher's hands and said, "I just want to forgive myself and I want forgiveness". He led me through this prayer and I clung to every word he spoke and I repeated it word for word. All of a sudden...

JESUS. I met Him! My body felt light and peaceful. It felt like electricity jolted me. I cried and cried. It was the most amazing, transformational experience that I have ever known. Changed from dark to light, instantly. I was so on fire from that moment. I went home to my parents' house. I told them. My dad said to me, "I thought you'd already done this".

My life has never been the same since that day. It's only getting better! From glory to glory and freedom to freedom . . . I'm going home. It was not easy. If it hadn't been for my friend, Dawn, I would have been completely alone. Not a single ally. I was excited and full of energy and zeal. I tried to save everyone. I was testing God at every single turn and He gave me all that I needed. He was my all in all. I was so on fire and hungry. I didn't sleep much because I was so hungry for the word. I read and read and read . . . all through the night. I am filled up to the rim with the word of God.

I went to church, came home, and went to work. Life moves on. One mistake after another. A few years after my first marital mistake, there was another one. This is a year and a half after I met Jesus. I'm living with my parents. I'm not seeing a bright future. I'm lonely and I'm ready to settle for less. I met a guy. Months go by, he proposed.

As soon as I put that ring on my finger, I felt sick. My chest hurt. I was miserable. I was absolutely miserable for 3 days. After the 3rd day - I took it off and called everything off. As soon as I took that ring off, I was in perfect peace. I told him, I need time and a break and I'm not at peace.

A few days went by and he called, crying and miserable. I caved. Not because I loved him but I didn't see any other way for myself to get out of the situation that I was in. I married him. I knew that it was wrong. I knew that I was being disobedient to God. I knew it. I did it anyway.

Guess where we ended up? Did you guess divorce court? ***You nailed it!*** The only thing good that came out of that mess was my oldest daughter. We'll talk more about that later. I'm really just trying to give you an idea of where I'm coming from.

I hate to call these 2 relationships marriage because it just doesn't feel honoring to my amazing husband, Aaron. I was desperate. I had no guidance at all. I was an orphan and didn't see any value in myself at all. I was tired of what religion had placed on me my entire life and especially now that I was a born again Christian with 2 divorces on my record. Now - I was really tainted and scarlet.

I walked away. No one spoke Grace. No one spoke Mercy. I was done and I wanted nothing else to do with the church. They let me down. No phone calls. No visits. Nothing. I was a nobody, drifting away into nothing.

I did the only thing I knew to do… I drowned myself at work. I was good at it and I loved it. I left everything and everyone and gave myself to work.

I drowned all of my problems in my career and learned how to quickly skim the surface of life. I was getting more and more numb, every day. There was that loneliness again, so familiar, coming in waves of grief that I could not prevent, and so I worked harder. I didn't have time to think about my future and I was too tired to do anything else.

Here begins my prodigal journey. It was 7 years long. I was doing the best I could to raise my little girl. It was hard and I quit wishing that I could get that part of my life back. It wasn't wasted. It was hard and lonely and dry. It was expensive and taxing and the worst part of it all was what it did to my little girl.

I loved Rachel but I was broken. I was a mess. I was completely alone. I find myself looking into her prodigal journey now. It breaks my heart. I know God is wooing her just like He did me. He never gave up. He came to me in dreams and He protected me. He was there and I still don't understand that. He was there in the shadows. He kept me from harm and He kept me on many specific occasions from being harmed.

I worked for a pizza chain and met this guy at a business meeting. I wasn't interested in this guy and never showed any interest. At some point I quit the chain and went on to another place of business. Somehow he found me. He was calling me at work and I stopped taking his calls at work after the first time I said don't call me. He then started showing up at my job. Over and over again he was coming in and just lurking around.

One day - he wasn't there. I'd been told that he was coming in and asking people questions about me and following me around. He had a history of sexual assault. I did not know this until later. Someone told me that he died during surgery, a simple procedure but he died on the operating table. I took that very seriously.

I missed my heavenly Father. I missed "home". I was lonely and the only place that I ever felt like I belonged was with Him. It was my 30th birthday and I knew that was the day that I needed to grow up. I had made a mess since the last time He and I had really spent any quality time together. My heart, my soul, my entire life was a dry desert. I was nothing without Him. I wanted nothing but to go home! I saw God run . . . . He was running to rescue me!

I spent my 30th birthday alone, by choice. I hadn't really cried in years and wasn't sure I could. A lot had happened and I was older. I had walls around my heart and really didn't know what to expect. I sat on the edge of my bed . . . I said, "Abba, I miss you - can I come home." I slid down the side of my bed and curled my knees up and the tears came. I wept.

And I came home . . . .

Chapter 3

Niagara Falls 2004

I worked 2 jobs and was a single mother. I was so tired and knew that I didn't have the capacity to move on nor any hope for life itself. I was done. My restaurant career has ended and I didn't know what else to do. I was completely alone in life with no direction and not a friend in the world. I was as lost as a man on the open seas without a sail and no compass. I knew that I was done if God did not come through for me.

I lived in a little, one bedroom apartment in London, Ohio. It was small, cute and very lonely. I would sit in the window sill at night with nothing better to do than to watch the drunks cross the street and fight each other while I was smoking a cigarette and drinking a beer.

I came home late one night after working all day and evening, walked through my front door, fell to my knees and cried out. I threw my ball cap on the ground and said to God . . . "I can't do this anymore. I am done. If you have someone for me, you'd better bring him. If not - make this work because I can't do this anymore. I'm finished!"

2 months later I met my husband. We met in August and were married exactly 3 months later. I do not recommend anyone ever do this without the prompting of Holy Spirit. Trust me - it was not easy. Stay with me while I tell you the story of what God did for my hard heart.

Before I met Aaron, I had a plan. Somehow, I knew that I was going to Niagara Falls but I had no idea why, how or when.

I met Aaron through a website called Christian Mingle. It is a dating website and also for like minded believers to get together for coffee, biking, whatever your hobby might be. Aaron had the trial membership and of course I bought the lifetime membership. I had absolutely no faith at all about meeting anyone, much less ever getting married.

I came across his faceless profile and was drawn to it because he mentioned the Holy Spirit. I knew that he must have some depth to him and so I gave him a little note that said, nice smile. We interacted for a couple of days until his membership ran out and then we swapped emails. We emailed back and forth. In fact - I just told Aaron that I'd give anything to have those emails.

My brother had tickets to go see the Newsboys and he invited me. I said that I'd go but only because I had no life. It was true, I was a workaholic and had no life at all. Can you believe that my brother ditched me? He got called into work and had to cancel. He gave me the tickets... like who am I going to take?!

I invited Aaron and he graciously accepted. Neither of us had any idea what we were getting into. We've never even met! I didn't know what he looked like but he knew how to recognize me based on my profile pictures on that social website. He sent pictures and I saw that he had blue eyes and all of his teeth. The date was on.

The day was upon us and it was date night. I don't think I was nervous or scared at all but I was pretty tough and held a great poker face. I didn't carry a lot of emotion at this time in my life. I arrived and the parking lot was full of cars. To give you an idea of how many cars and people there were - it was August and we were attending the Ohio State Fair. The concert was there on the fairgrounds.

I arrived and he wasn't there. No phone call or anything. Just like I expected, he stood me up. No skin off my back, I had nothing invested in this at all. An hour later, he calls. He's here! I walked to the entrance and as I turned the corner he literally ran into me. Sparks didn't fly but he was so nervous and I was, well, me. I punched him on the arm gently and said, "you're late . . come on." I walked about 10 paces in front as he followed along. He was so quiet. Have you seen the movie "Up"? If you have, I'm Ellie and he's Carl.

We got in and got to our seats. The most powerful thing about him that night was the way he worshiped God. I'd never seen that before. He was a man, with me, with his arms raised in worship of our God. We enjoyed that space together and worshiped God.

When the concert was over, we stayed and walked around and talked. We shared and laughed and rode rides and closed down the fair that night. We walked to our cars and he, being the gentleman that he is, walked me to mine. We swapped numbers and decided that we would talk again. The closer we got to my car - he realized that he had parked right next to me. Out of 100's possibly 1000's of cars, he parked right next to me! That was crazy, but honestly, no crazier than anything else that's happened in our life together.

We said goodbye and drove off. He followed behind me. I called him up and asked him if he'd like to go to the Waffle House and grab coffee. He said yes! I don't know how long we were there but it was late. We finally decided that we should probably say goodnight. He walked me to my car and said . . "Welp, let's stay in touch." I don't know why but that comment seemed cheap. I said . . . "what?" He said…"I will call you." He told me that he had plans with a buddy and so he'd call me in a few days. He called me the next day and came to see me that very next night. The rest is History! We dated and ate out and danced and walked and shopped and finally, I got my trip to Niagara Falls!

The Romance . . . .

God drew us into a grand story that He had already written, but we were only just beginning to discover.

My daughter, Rachel, was in Tennessee when I met Aaron. It was the end of August and time to drive to Kentucky to pick her up. Aaron and I had just spent a couple of weeks together dating and getting to know one another a little bit. It was fun and I liked this guy!

Our focus was Christ alone. We spent our time talking, rejoicing and worshiping. It really was an amazing time and I was sure that this might be the guy - but I was not saying a word.

Before I met Aaron I had it in my head that I was going to go to Niagara Falls and take my daughter. I still have the newspaper that my friend gave to me at the time. It was just a story about Niagara Falls. I was going - come hell or high water. When Aaron and I first started dating, I told him that. He said . . . "ok, I'll go with you!" I had no idea that God was setting us up!

We picked Rachel up that month and she met Aaron for the first time. When she got in the car, we talked and asked questions. She (very out of character for her) said, "stop talking"! She said, "I just want to talk about Jesus"! We stopped and waited. She said that she wanted Jesus in her heart and she wanted to ask now. She did that without any help from us. That was amazing! Rachel's spiritual birthday is in August 2004. That was the best road trip I remember ever having, up to that point in my life.

We finally completed our trip planning and were off! It was an amazing trip. It was exciting and I honestly had no idea what we were facing. I was just ready to go! We worshipped and prayed together all the way there. We shared stories and laughed. At some point during the trip, I was delivered from something that I had struggled with for years! We were surrounded by God's holy Presence and things had already begun to fall off, in the car! Boy was God setting us up for success!

We finally got to the border and got into our place. It was a 4 day trip but it felt like time stood still for us. We reserved a room at a bed and breakfast. I think the owner made a mistake and we ended up getting an entire house next to the bed and breakfast. How awesome! We each got our own bedroom and the entire house to ourselves! We were within walking distance to the falls and all of downtown. It was so incredible.

Aaron spoiled us rotten those few days. There were so many things, little things that just kept happening. Even the music that played on the radio was so perfect and surreal. We pulled into the driveway of the place that we were staying and were just about ready to get out of the car and a song came on. Rachel had fallen asleep. The song is called "Godsend". The first few words are . . . Hoping, praying . . .I've been waiting . . . everybody needs somebody to love. We stopped, listened and embraced that moment. It felt like time literally stopped for us.

Our first 2 nights there we did not sleep much at all. Our hearts were being stirred and we just wanted to be in every moment as much as possible. We prayed, danced, talked and laughed the nights away. I remember being scared out of my mind. Things with Aaron and I seemed to be moving so fast. I was sitting with Aaron one night and I told God, "I'm scared". I heard the Holy Spirit whisper to me, "you can trust him."

Those words carried me through the next several years when my world came crumbling down. With every trigger and every demonic accusation, I would remember what God said… "You can trust him!" I can trust him! That became my mantra.

It was a weekend that most people have never been able to experience and I almost didn't. I am thankful that I did. It changed the course of my life and I have never been the same.

And, here's another really amazing moment that I will never forget. We were standing under the falls. There were other people everywhere. I stood under the falls with the roaring, deafening falls and the pose with my hands and arms raised to worship God. I sang at the top of my voice and not a single person heard me!

Aaron and I dedicated our relationship and everything around it to God and because of that we have been healed, delivered and very blessed. Though it took quite some time to walk out the healing journey, God has been so faithful. That is the advice that I would give to anyone and everyone who plans to be married. I said marriage . . . .

(Aaron's response)...

It was a scary time for both of us. I was bound up and scared, coming from a broken place in my own life before I met Jen. The miracle of being parked right next to her car in a lot of thousands of cars is real. After we finished the Newsboys concert, we both laughed when we discovered that I had "accidentally" parked right next to her car!

What's really cool looking back, is that our daughter, Linda Grace, (we call her "Gracie") has a favorite Christian Band and guess who it is… "The Newsboys!" We had no influence there and never really listen to them at home, but I find it very interesting that out of all the bands that Gracie could decide to like, she chose the Newsboys… the same band and music Jen and I listened to when we had our first unofficial date.

I was bound up and afraid when I met Jen. I was so afraid that I thought that we might be doing the wrong thing, meeting and being together. However, as 2 terrified adult kids with a lot of baggage, we took 1 day at a time and by His favor, we kept being drawn to each other.

When we went to Niagara Falls, we honored each other and neither of us had ever been so overwhelmed and romanced by God as we were during that 4 day trip. It seemed to last forever. We both knew we were in way over our heads, but it was His goodness that we were drowning in for the first time in our lives… we knew that He was up to something really good and that we were meant to be together.

Chapter 4

Getting Married

Aaron and I knew that marriage was inevitable. We were scared to death, but it was what we wanted. God was calling us to go deeper with Him. Healing was necessary and it had to come through marriage.

Aaron had a pure heart for me and was so dedicated to seeing me free. I wish he were here to tell you what he saw. I was so locked up. I had only lived in a shallow place all my life. I shut down almost completely as a child in order to survive and had no idea how to bring my soul back to life. I was a survivor but little did I know I was about to become an overcomer.

My parents moved to Alabama. Looking back, that was necessary. I don't think I could have made room for healing with them close to me. We packed them up and Aaron helped move their things to a storage unit in Tennessee.

The abuse that I had encountered as a child was horrific and because of the severity of it and how long I was being abused I shut down very early on in my life.

As a child my mantra had become… it's bad now but it will end soon. This will all be over soon and then I escaped in my little mind and heart. I honestly don't know where I went but I discovered many years later that it has caused a split in my person. I was never diagnosed with anything, I just knew that something was wrong.

When I married Aaron I fell completely apart. I wasn't expecting to fall into a deep and dark depression but I did.

Aaron began praying for me while we were dating and he was told that as he prayed for me it's likely I would begin to fall apart. I did.

The undoing was more than either of us could handle. The first few years of our marriage was so scary. We fought, cried, screamed, cried and fought some more throughout the first few years of our marriage. I was definitely going through an undoing or an unraveling.

I want to really encourage you that you will get through these dark and painful times. The very fact that you feel pain means that you are coming back to life! I fell into a depression because my heart was waking up. I was experiencing feelings that I had never felt before. I was being loved and beginning to love back. I was terrified!

We have been married for a couple of decades now and everything that we went through was worth it. I am so thankful that he stayed with me and that I stayed the course. Our faithful friend, Jesus, helped us, saved us over and over and loved us so well all the way through every single situation.

We suffered a lot of loss during this time. People walked away from us because we were just too messy and a few, very few, stayed with us until they were released. I am so thankful for those who left. They missed a huge blessing but it made room for those who stayed.

As you unravel just remember that there is light at the end of the tunnel. This, too, shall pass and you are not alone though you feel so lonely.

I remember feeling crazy and so ashamed. I felt so alone and I felt so much pain and thought I wanted to die.

But I held my ground. I believed God even when I did not. I lifted my heart and my life to Him, asking and waiting for my healing.

God loved me so deeply through my husband and bringing me patience, gentleness, love and kindness all along the way. It is exactly what I needed but it was not easy for him.

Chapter 5

A Word for Your Spouse

A word for your spouse: please don't give up. She is worth it. And please don't give up on yourself because you are worth it. Don't put a time limit on her healing because that is not entirely within your control. God will help you when you feel out of control. He will help you when you don't have the answers. He will help you when you feel like you are losing everything, including the beautiful wife that you dreamed of spending the rest of your life with.

When I married Aaron, I fell apart. I fell into a deep depression and I felt so out of control in the earlier part of our marriage.

I did not understand what triggers were, but I do now! I was triggered at every corner. This was terrifying to me, my new husband, my daughter, and a few people in our church family . . .

I was so ashamed. I wanted to run and hide and at some point, I just wanted to die. I prayed for my life to end!

When I met Aaron, I guess I hadn't realized the extent of my emotional numbness. I had no idea, really, until my heart began to wake up; experiencing love for the first time, and also being loved purely. I didn't know what to do with what was happening inside of me.

I became afraid and fearful of Aaron's love. I was afraid of being abandoned, cheated on, or physically harmed. I was afraid of losing control. I needed to know every little detail. I was hyper vigilant and very controlling and very filled with rage. I was a walking time bomb, not knowing when I was going to go off.

As you walk through healing, you will need to be very patient and you will need Jesus to help you through this. There is no way that your marriage (and possibly you) will survive this without the King of kings.

Though it is hard, it is possible.

"Ah, Sovereign LORD, you have made the heavens and the earth by your great power and outstretched arm. Nothing is too hard for you." (Jeremiah 32:17 NIV)

"I am the LORD, the God of all mankind. Is anything too hard for me?" (Jeremiah 32:27 NIV)

Jesus looked at them and replied, "With people it is impossible, but not with God — God makes all things possible!' (Mark 10:27 TPT)

"Do you think there is anything too marvelous for Yahweh? I will appear to you at the appointed time next year and Sarah will have a son!" (Genesis 18:14 TPT)

"For no word from God will ever fail." (Luke 1:37 NIV)

Come on! Our God is faithful. He is the Faithful One. Not you, not me. My friend said to me yesterday while sitting at her table, "it's a new day". That landed on me hard! So I am going to give that to you!

Friend, today is a new day! And our Redeemer is making all things new! ALL!!!

Activation:

Breathe. Relax. Let Him. Let Jesus love you. Trust Him and when you don't, ask Him to help you. Beloved, you are loved.

Prayer for spouse of survivor:

Jesus,
I didn't know all the pain they were carrying when we fell in love.
I couldn't see the weight of what was buried,
the scars that didn't show,
the wounds from long ago that still bleed quietly today.

But You knew.
And You chose me to walk beside them in this holy, hard healing.
And so I come to You—not with all the answers,
but with a heart that's open.

Teach me how to love gently.
Give me discernment to know when to speak and when to be silent.
Help me to listen, not to fix—
To hold space, not pressure—
To be present, even when I don't understand.

Heal what I cannot reach.
Restore what I cannot rebuild.
Be the safety they've never known.
Be the peace that steadies them when the past comes back uninvited.

When the journey feels long and I grow tired,
remind me that love is patient.
When fear whispers that I'm not enough,
remind me that Your grace is.

Give me courage to stay when things feel confusing.
Give me eyes to see them not as damaged—but as deeply brave.
Let me reflect Your love, Your compassion, and Your steadiness.
And may our home be a sanctuary—where shame has no voice,
and healing has room to breathe.

I can't rescue them, Jesus. But You can.
I can't rewrite their past. But You can redeem it.
Use me—not as a savior, but as a servant of love.
Not to lead, but to walk with.
Not to fix, but to stand in faith.

Thank You for trusting me with their heart.
I offer it back to You—again and again.
Keep it safe in Your hands. - Amen

Chapter 6

Women

Many years ago I was fearful of being close to women or even sharing space with them. I didn't trust them. They were every woman that my abusers gawked at. They were every woman who knew I was being abused but stood by and did nothing. They were every woman that I was ever compared to. I hated women, including myself.

But…

I was so lonely. I craved authentic relationships so badly but I was so afraid. I was afraid that if I got close, they would see me. I was afraid if they got close that my husband would do what everyone else did, betray me, compare me, leave me.

And so I stayed away becoming aware of my triggers and how hypervigilant I was. I was living in a bubble that was about to explode.

I had a dream one night that I was riding on a horse and we were running towards a city and there were women and young women everywhere. I was running with them. But there was a tree growing right in the center of the horse.

The tree was representative to what was getting in the way and it blinded me.

Over the years God removed that tree, the LOG. And I have become more and more free to run with the horses.

I have been walking in discovery for many years about what Jeremiah 12:5 means to me and for my life as a Daughter. I think I want to share with you what my eyes were opened to today.

Jeremiah was rebuked by the Lord because he was being impatient. God said to Jeremiah, 'if you can't endure your community coming against you, how will you endure the persecution of the nations?"

There will be times when even the believers in your community will betray you, reject you, abandon you.

Is God enough?

He is and we have to come to that reality because we will be betrayed and rejected by those in our church community and those in our own family will come after us, pursue us. That can look like gossip, slander, withholding affection, ghosting us…

It hurts. I am fully aware. I am also becoming more aware that it doesn't matter. Though they leave me, He will never forsake me or reject me.

I am learning from the Master, Jesus. I am learning and am comforted by Holy Spirit. I am fathered by Abba. I am never alone because He has set me in the heavenlies where every answer to every problem also exists.

Who counsels you?

Who fathers you?

Where do you go for encouragement? Where do you go for comfort? Do you go outward or just inward to stuff your problems?

Or do you look to the Lord for where your help comes from?

"I lift up my eyes to the hills-- where does my help come from? My help comes from the LORD, the Maker of heaven and earth. Indeed, he who watches over Israel will neither slumber nor sleep. the sun will not harm you by day, nor the moon by night." (Psalms 121: 1-6 NIV)

Activation

Close your eyes. Turn off the noise. What do you hear? What voice are you listening to?

Hone in on the one voice of your Shepherd. Do you hear Him? What is He saying?

John 10: 27 (TPT) says: "My own sheep will hear my voice and I know each one, and they will follow me."

There is no life that you can possibly imagine that is as good as the life that He has planned for you.

Prayer

Jesus, You know how deeply I've been hurt by women.
The ones who were supposed to protect me, love me, stand beside me—some of them wounded me instead.
I've carried that pain quietly. I've smiled through betrayal and pain.
I've shut the doors of my heart to keep other women out.
But now I see that I've also locked myself in.

I don't want to live guarded anymore.
I want to trust —in friendship, in sisterhood, in the promise of safe connection.
But I need Your help, Lord.

Teach me how to discern what is healthy.
Lead me into authentic relationships with women who are whole and healing.
Help me to let go of bitterness. Give me wisdom.

I forgive the women who betrayed me.
Not because it didn't hurt,
Not because it was okay,
But because I refuse to carry their brokenness in my body any longer.

Heal the places in me that are still suspicious, still scared, still cynical.
Heal the little girl in me who didn't feel picked, protected, or believed.
Surround me with women who are kind, truthful, Spirit-filled, and pure-hearted.

Give me courage to show up again—slowly, gently, wisely.
Even if my hands tremble.
Even if my voice shakes.
I will not hide forever.

I declare that I will see goodness in the land of the living.
I will find safe women.
I will be a safe woman.
And I will not do life alone.

Amen.

Chapter 7

Memories

A long time ago I spent some time thinking about all of the people in my life, good and bad. I decided to make a timeline of every person and every event that I could remember. It was so healing to me - It has helped me on multiple occasions, reconcile so many memories and relationships. It has also helped me to look for the good.

Often when we were abused as children, the bad really sticks out. And listen, don't discount the good memories even if the same person ended up being sour to you later in life. That is very common with scapegoats. If you were a victim of abuse, you were most likely a scapegoat.

I'm sharing this to give you a practical processing activity that will help you reconcile and redeem the good from your past.

I have done this process and similar projects like this multiple times, and have led many others through it, including my family.

The feedback has always been redemptive. Everyone who has done this has mined some real gold in their past, even out of the depths of dark memories.

And, if you want to get poster boards and markers to work on this project, feel free. That's how I like to do it, especially when I lead this in groups.

To begin, go back as far as you can and start with the very first person that you can remember.

For me, it's my mother. Though I don't have a deep relationship with her now, I have fond memories of her and she taught me some things that I am thankful for.

Next are my grandparents! Oh, I smile when I go back to those days. I had the most wonderful grandfather. He had the best laugh and the sweetest eyes towards me.

Are you starting to get the picture?

Don't hold back. There is something very final and beautiful and redemptive about this little project.

Ask God to bring back good memories and redeem the bad. He will do it. He has such a beautiful plan for your life. His intentions are good towards you.

When you are ready, I'd love to hear from you. I'd like to hear your stories and your testimony of what God has been able to do for you.

I hope that I make it to that timeline and that my testimony has been a catalyst in your life. I hope that when you close this book and have read every last word that you will be more free than before. Not because I can unbind you or save you but because you've seen that you are not alone and what Christ has done for me, He can and will do for you.

You just have to let Him.

As we wrap up and come to an end in this part of our journey, I want to say thank you.

This has been so hard and so emotional for me to write my story on these pages, while doing my best to honor everyone involved. Tell the truth and honor others. That's what my spiritual father told me just before he passed from this life.

Our testimonies are not a waste.

They are both precious and bloody. And they do not belong just to us. No one has ever suffered the way Christ has and He understands everything that you have suffered and He knows what you are going through now. He loves you and is not afraid of any of our messes.

I am leaving you a gift.

There is a list for you to read over the person that you see in the mirror. I will leave it with you, trusting God to fulfill His promises in your life. I also believe that someday you will believe what He says about you.

Please believe me when I tell you… you are seen and heard, needed and wanted, loved, trusted and valuable.

Until we meet at the restoration of all things . . . I love you, friend.

Activation

For this one, find a mirror. Stay. Even if it hurts. Stay and begin to speak life over her. You might have to repeat this over a period of days, weeks, or months.

"You are loved. You are precious. Your life has meaning. You are not alone. I love you. I LOVE YOU. I love ME. I am God's Daughter. I am free. I am His Beloved. I am His Darling. I still have a lot of good work to do. I have become God's poetry."

Scripture to ponder - Ephesians 2:10, John 15:12, Romans 8:28, Jeremiah 29:11

God wants to redeem every memory.

Chapter 8

Sometimes Things Break

I was driving somewhere the other day. I needed to be in my car. I needed free space to think and to hear something from Jesus. Jesus spoke to my dry soul that day. I needed to just "be".

I turned on Pandora and let whatever was next stream through my car speaker. I had never heard this song before. I love Stephanie Gretzinger. I wasn't expecting to hear the words that streamed through. They fell right into my soul.

Sometimes things break.

When I heard those words . . . the dam broke. They hit my soul like a feather. Touching me exactly where I needed to be touched.

Words.

I have a love-hate relationship with words. I guess it depends on the words that are spilling over. I'm not good at guarding my heart, yet. I'm better - not great.

That particular morning, I was beating myself up. I am very hard on myself, at times, and I don't want to be. I think most people are, especially women. Jesus is pressing in on me there. He is so good at loving me through my family and a few people that I let close.

He is so good at loving. Isn't He?

As these words washed my mind and my soul, I could feel His breath on me. I could hear His whisper:

> *Sometimes things break.*
>
> *You're growing and learning and sometimes things break, sometimes stars fall from the sky.*
>
> *Look at me. Look at me.*

I will hold you. I will never break. I will never break you.

I will love you.

I know you and I get you. I know why you do what you do. I know why and I know what you need, when you need it.

Sometimes things break but I never will. I will always catch your heart. I will hold you. I will give you all that you need.

At the end of the day, after things break, did you love? Were you loved?

At the end of the day, love is all that lasts. Did you love? Were you loved?"

Remembering that sometimes things break is the most encouraging thing in my world.

It's ok.

I don't need to fix what broke. I don't need to worry about what broke. I can cry and grieve. Maybe what broke was a good thing. Sometimes good things . . . break. And when it does, it hurts.

Why do we try so hard to hold things together? Why is it so important what others think about us? Why do we strive to protect what is broken? Why do we feel the pressure to not let others see what is broken in our lives? Maybe it's the shame of the brokenness. Maybe it's guilt.

Last night I was going through some old letters and cards from past friends and leaders. They are so valuable and no amount of money could ever replace the words. Many of these cards and letters spoke right into where I am today. The words became life and grew inside of my soul and have manifested. Many of them I am now walking in.

And then I remembered another spoken word, spoken over me countless times. At the time, it felt so good to be seen as strong and totally together. The words were,

"You are strong. You are stronger than her or him."

I remembered these words last night as I glimpsed through cards from pastors and leaders. It felt like a gut punch. I was able to forgive the people that put this kind of pressure on me and move on. These are very well meaning people who just say things that they haven't thought through very well.

Little did they know that I was falling apart and coming completely undone on the inside.

I was not strong and I was just as fragile as anyone else, maybe more. I needed permission to fall apart. I needed permission to not be strong. I needed permission to let go of all that was broken but instead I was expected to be strong. I picked up strengths and masks and carried on. I held it together when other people were around. I put on whatever mask fit the situation. I was fading. I was dying. I was sinking deeper and deeper until I lost all sense of who I might be.

Sometimes things break.

Sometimes stars fade.

Sometimes relationships end.

Sometimes we fall.

Sometimes we lose.

Sometimes we break.

Today, I am thankful that Jesus gave me permission to ***not*** hold it together.

He has given me permission to no longer be strong, to fall, to fail, to break. Jesus gave me permission to take off every mask. He has given me permission to throw off all of my strength. He has given me permission to let go of what is broken.

The voice of religion will tell you, scream at you . . . NO.

Hold it together!

And it will even throw scripture in your face.

Instead… stand your ground. Listen to the gentle voice of Jesus and let go. There is freedom just beyond.

I open up my hands and let go. I breathe in and accept that sometimes things break. I feel like I can breathe when I let go. No longer looking at every little broken piece and trying to put them together. I feel happy that I don't need to be strong. I feel ok with letting you see my broken pieces and I find hope in knowing that one person will be encouraged by reading this.

I can see you, breathing in, closing your eyes and breathing out. I can see the tears that have built up over the years, staining your face.

Finally someone is giving you permission to let go.

Open your hands, blow those broken pieces into the air. Let them go. Close your eyes and breathe.

Do you feel that?

I just prayed for you. You now have permission to ***not*** be strong and to take off your mask.

You have permission to grieve.

You have permission to be angry and to hurt over what has been broken.

Sometimes things break . . . .

Chapter 9

Depleted & Lonely

I have felt a deep loneliness in my life…

I didn't understand why I have always felt so alone or why I didn't have any friends. Maybe this is how cliques can make people feel. I've seen circles of people around me, but I've never truly been part of them. And then I realized—it's always been that way.

This morning I was reminded of the depth of my loneliness. I was rehearsing every relationship and how they all seemed like they have failed in some way. Thinking about how it feels… i.e. the only time I see people is if I reach out, or if someone wants something from me.

Who is my friend?

Jesus - He is a friend of mine.

When I feel this way, I need to look into His eyes and I will know that He is my friend. When I just look into His eyes, I'll be reminded of who I am and that I have value. He will never leave me alone. He is always near and always wants to be with me.

I am valuable.

I am whole.

I am loved.

I am His alone.

I am not alone.

This is what I know when I look into His eyes.

I know who I am.

Activation

It's ok to not be invited. It's ok to refrain from reaching out to those who do not reciprocate a desire to be my friend. Look for one friend. I recommend a spiritual mother. Someone who will love you and speak truth to you in this season. Turn off all the other voices. Look at Jesus and believe that He is your friend in every season of your life.

Lord, fill me up. Fill me and encase me in your love right now. Speak Your better word over me. Remind me of your friendship when I am lonely and when I feel empty.

"Rise up and help us; rescue us because of your unfailing love." (Psalms 44:26 NIV)

"Hear my prayer, O God; listen to the words of my mouth." (Psalm 54:2 NIV)

Chapter 10

Grief and Love

Grief is hard - but necessary.

It's not just about death.

Grief comes after any loss, especially the loss of what could have been… what should have been. It comes when someone you loved hurt you so deeply, so repeatedly, that parts of you broke off just to survive.

And that's where the confusion lives:

Grieving someone who is still alive.
Grieving the version of them you hoped for.
Grieving the relationship that didn't exist.

Have you ever felt trapped between the love you once gave and the pain you now carry?

That place is excruciating - because you don't know what to do with what's still lingering in your heart. You still remember the good moments, but they're tangled in betrayal. You once trusted, but now you flinch. You once gave love freely, but now your soul is on lockdown.

That's grief too.

Especially when the one who hurt you… is someone you were supposed to feel safe with.

A parent. A spouse. A pastor. A friend.

Grief is the body's way of letting go of what your soul can no longer carry. And yet, we rarely give ourselves permission to grieve abusive relationships—because the lines get blurred.

"How can I still love them after what they did?"

"Why does this hurt so much when I know they were toxic?"

"Was any of it even real?"

This is the sacred tension of trauma:

You didn't ask for the pain. But you're still left to sort through the pieces.

Unless someone has been abused, they can't understand it.

No one can understand the weight of abuse unless they've walked through it. And if they haven't—they don't get to tell you how to carry your grief.

Survivors often feel pressured to stay silent. Fear of being misunderstood, judged, or dismissed keeps them isolated. What most people don't realize is how common this pain is—it just isn't spoken aloud.

I remember the unraveling years ago - trying to breathe through trauma while pretending I was okay. People around me couldn't grasp it.

"Hurry up and get better," they said.

"Be your old self again so we can hang out."

But healing doesn't come on command.

Today, I'm grateful. Grateful for the ones who stayed and walked with me gently. And strangely, grateful for the ones who didn't—because both taught me something I needed to know.

Authenticity Isn't Public. It's Personal.

Authentic living isn't about performing for people. It's not glass-house Christianity. It's about being real before the Lord - real with your grief, your pain, your process.

I used to think authenticity meant sharing every detail with everyone. But I learned the hard way—that's not wisdom. That's exposure.

Now, I keep my pearls close.

Jesus doesn't need you to perform your healing. He walks with you in it. Quietly. Closely. Faithfully.

Children remind me of this. They're honest. Unfiltered. They live with soft eyes and full hearts. I used to live that way too… until trauma hardened me. But healing taught me how to live in the light again.

When we bring our grief, our confusion, and our broken love to God—He meets us there. And healing begins, not when we have all the answers, but when we simply say:

Yes.

Even when it hurts.

Even when we don't understand.

Yes to the process.

Yes to Jesus.

Yes to healing.

Let the Healer heal!

Let Him.

Activation

Let Yourself Grieve

1. Name the Loss.

Is it the version of someone you hoped they would be?
Is it a relationship that ended without closure?
Is it innocence, trust, or safety that was stolen from you?

2. Let yourself feel it.

Write it out. Speak it in prayer. Cry if you need to. Just don't numb it. Don't rush it. Healing lives in honesty. Healing takes time.

3. Speak this out loud:

"I give myself permission to grieve what was lost—
and I give God permission to heal what still hurts."

Prayer

Jesus,

I'm hurting.

There's a deep grief in me—some of it I understand, some of it I don't. You know every place where love and pain have collided. You see what I've tried to carry alone.

Today, I give it to You. I give You my silence, my sadness, my confusion, my pain.

Heal the broken pieces in me. Help me live with soft eyes again. Teach me to trust You in the grief and to find comfort in Your presence.

I say yes to healing.

Even when it hurts.

Amen.

SECTION TWO: The Deep Work

This is where the pain starts talking—and where Jesus begins to whisper louder. These chapters dive into the tender, gritty process of confronting trauma, tending to the body, and surrendering the broken places we've tried to hide.

Chapter 11

Don't Downplay Your Pain

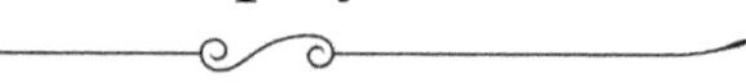

For many years I downplayed the pain that I felt in my soul. Until one day, my soul could no longer feel anything. No one was better at the "game" than me. I even quoted Paul. I said, "I can be all things to all people". Of course I took that out of its context to fit my life. I knew that I could match any personality in front of me. I was not intimidated by men or women and I did not care what hand I was given, I'd play cards with anyone.

Religion was my best game. I knew the scriptures. I knew how to "behave" inside of the church. But I also knew that I hated hypocrites and so I stayed out of the church for a long time. I didn't want to be accused of being one, a hypocrite that is. When I did go back to church, I discovered that I could jump into that scene easily. I was numb and hiding but no one had to know.

Until one day my heart began to wake up. The walls of hate began to break down and melt away until I started to "feel" love. I did not like that! It scared me! What was happening to me? It was so overwhelming that I fell into a deep depression.

I can remember like it was yesterday when that happened. The sadness was overwhelming and I desperately wanted to die. I asked God to end my life over and over. But He didn't, and I'm so glad!

I wasn't sure what to do with what was happening inside of me. In fact, no one knew what to do with me. Suddenly the game was changing. I wasn't able to play anymore but I couldn't give up so easily.

Our pastors and leaders in the church we were attending at the time kept passing me off to one another saying, "we don't know what to do with her". My behaviour was so sideways and I desperately needed help.

I was newly married and I can tell you that my husband was definitely unsure of what to do, not with me, but how to help me. And so he began to really lean into Jesus and depend on Him.

Jesus was our only hope.

Our church family literally abandoned us. It was so painful to me. Here are a few things that I heard.

1. "Hurry up and get better so that Aaron and I can hang out." I had severe separation anxiety and was terrified of rejection and betrayal. I clung to Aaron like a baby clings to a blanket.

2. "What's wrong with you? You've changed." I was changing and it was not pretty. I was in the boat with people who denied suffering and change and therefore what they were witnessing in my life was weird, sinful and something must have been very wrong with me.

3. "You are the strong one, Jen. You need to be the strong one for _____. What happened to you? You used to evangelize and bring people into the church." They didn't recognize my performer. They only saw what they wanted to see. I was a commodity to the church. They weren't willing to sit with us long enough to help, to walk with us, to see us restored.

4. "We do not have what it takes to help you." They did if they were filled with the Spirit of God but were unwilling to get dirty.

5. "This church is not for everyone." I agree. It was more of a social club and we left when we no longer felt the Spirit of God wanting us to remain in that church.

I'll stop there. Are you triggered? I kind of feel like my face is burning and my heartbeat is beating a little faster than usual.

Listen. I'm so sorry. I am so sorry that this has happened to you.

Let's go back to embracing what we have gone through. Let's talk more about downplaying our pain.

I picked up a book once and I can't remember the title to save my life, but it changed the game for me. Don't downplay your pain. Instead, hold hands with it.

It didn't make sense to me at first because I lived in denial for all of my life.

Embrace what has happened to me!? That's everything that I have not learned!

As I began to accept what had happened to me, I was able to actually agree that it was not my fault. It was NOT my fault, It was not YOUR fault!

I would like to walk you through to help you embrace what happened to you so that you can acknowledge that it wasn't your fault. And also, to embrace that you really do feel pain and it is no longer ok to downplay it.

If you are in a community of people that care more about your performance than your healing, I want to ask you to remove yourself from that for a while.

It's hard. I get it. But I know that if God can deliver me and set me free, He will help you too. His love for you does not come with conditions. He has given everything for you to be able to walk in complete and perfect healing. You only need to just "let Him". He will show you the way.

Lord Jesus, I want to pray for your beloved child who is holding this book right now. I pray that You will make Your voice the loudest one to their ears. Give her courage to step out of religion and performance. Open her eyes to the next thing and give her courage to walk in that. I ask you to send Godly sisters and brothers and highlight them. I pray that you will accelerate her healing.

Oh, how I wish I knew your name darling. I am praying for you as you heal. Let yourself fall apart and trust the One who wants to rebuild you. He can put all the pieces back together for you when no one else can.

We can't allow people who do not have His love to walk with us. Not yet. There will be a day for that. You will be healed and whole and walk with people just like you. They will learn about Abba's love for you because of how He has healed you. You are special and will walk in a special way that is setting you apart.

Don't give up.

Activation

Take a deep breath. Breathe in and breathe out. Slowly. Breathe in and breathe out. Lift up your hands and just breathe. Say . . . Jesus. Say it again. Say it again and again. Be still.

Can you feel that? And now . . . though you might not trust Him. You will. Picture your pain in your hands that are lifted up. Can you see all that pain?

Say to Jesus, "Jesus, I give You all this pain that I feel so deeply. I don't understand it. But I am willing to trust You and give it all to You. I acknowledge my pain, my hurts and I need You. I need Your help.

"Trust in the Lord completely,
and do not rely on your own opinions.
With all your heart rely on him to guide you,
and he will lead you in every decision you make.
Become intimate with him in whatever you do,
and he will lead you wherever you go." (Proverbs 3:5-6 TPT)

"Stop imitating the ideals and opinions of the culture around you, but be inwardly transformed by the Holy Spirit through a total reformation of how you think. This will empower you to discern God's will as you live a beautiful life, satisfying and perfect in his eyes." (Romans 12:2 TPT)

Chapter 12

Do You Want to Be Healed?

I can never forget the despair that I was in when my healing journey began.

I was so desperate. I wanted to be "fixed". I wanted to be made new. I wanted my soul pain to stop. I wanted the torment to stop! I tried working, partying, smoking, working and then working some more. I was a workaholic. It felt good to focus on something that I was good at and then be really good at it. It felt good to work myself into the ground and fall into bed exhausted. I was completely numb until the nightmares came.

When Aaron and I got married, I felt little to nothing. I didn't know how to unlock feelings, good feelings and good emotions. I was so emotionally broken and spiritually broken and I was very aware and very ashamed of that. I kept my heart closed and close to me.

Aaron was the one to love me to healing when He partnered with Jesus. It was my husband's obedience that healed me. It was not easy.

I remember when we were first married and how emotionally overwhelmed I became when deep things began to resurface, and I was forced out of hiding. I had a dream about my heart during this season and God showed me flowers and a beautiful garden. He said, "I am waking your heart up to love".

I was in a tremendous amount of pain. I carried shame and wasn't sure how to get to where I wanted to be. The emotional pain of revisiting childhood trauma was worse than the actual traumatic events.

I asked God to end my life, over and over and over. I felt so lost and so out of control but He knew what I was really asking. I was really asking Him, "please help". I didn't trust Him. I wasn't sure about this whole "father in the sky" thing. I was good with Jesus but I did not want, nor did I need, a dad.

One day Jesus asked me, "do you want to be healed"? I said yes! He said . . . stretch out your hands. And I did.

The most childlike and dangerous thing that I ever said was - do whatever it takes . . . . I am going to trust You. This was the beginning of a beautiful, scary, dangerous, intimate and powerful journey. And I am so glad that I said yes.

There is always something required from us in order for healing and inner transformation to take place. God was not going to just come in uninvited and wreck me. That's exactly why I was in the shape I was in! He wanted my yes and my commitment.

John 5:6 is a perfect example of that. When Jesus saw him lying there and learned that he had been in this condition for a long time, he asked him, "Do you want to get well?"

Let me ask you. Do YOU want to be healed? Do you really want to get well? It will require something from you.

I have met so many men and women while on my journey that have said they want to be healed but they weren't willing to put in the effort. Oftentimes we feel comfortable with what we know and sometimes it's the pain we are in. That was me for a long time. I knew how to maneuver and manipulate in order to protect myself. I knew who and what and where to avoid. It was safe for me to remain broken.

When God begins healing our hearts the walls come down. The hard skin comes off and we begin to feel things that we never have before and that is terrifying! We aren't able to trust an unseen God for crying out loud. How can I when I wasn't able to protect myself from those that I could see!?

There have been times in my life as a sojourner when I could only muster up a prayer like this, "help". That is the most powerful and effective prayer that I have ever prayed.

I would like to ask you to do this one thing, for you, for those who love you and mostly for YOU…

Let Him.

I know how you feel. I know that it is so scary. I know that you aren't good at trusting. I know the pain that you feel. I know that what people did to you was wrong and horrible. But I also know the power of Jesus's blood and all that it can do. I know that healing is for you, too.

Jesus loves you and He cares for you. He cares about what you have been through and He wept because it was not supposed to be this way. You were created to know His love.

Here's something that I did to help me along. I would like for you to do this same thing.

Lift your precious hands to Him and offer Him your pain. And just stay there. That's all for now.

There is a beautiful grace on you as you heal. Just stay. Rest and stay and let Him.

Activation

Close your eyes and allow yourself to feel whatever it is that you are feeling. Feel it deep. Is it good, bad? Painful? Joyful? If you are ready and willing, let His question echo through your soul. Are you willing to be healed? When you are ready to offer your yes . . . lift your hands and give him your most honest and bold yes. And let Him.

Lord, encourage me in the yes. Let me just touch the hem of Your garment. Help me have a yes tomorrow, the next day, the next day. I will trust You. I will look for hope. I will believe You. I will lie down in green pastures.

Scriptures

When Jesus saw him lying there and learned that he had been in this condition for a long time, he asked him, "Do you want to get well?" (John 5:6 NIV)

In the crowd that day was a woman who had suffered greatly for twelve years from slow bleeding. Even though she had spent all that she had on healers, she was still suffering. Pressing in through the crowd, she came up behind Jesus and touched the fringe of his garment. Instantly her bleeding stopped and she was healed. Jesus suddenly stopped and said to his disciples, "Someone touched me. Who was it?" While they all denied it, Peter pointed out, "Master, everyone is touching you, trying to get close to you. The crowds are so thick we can't walk through all these people without being jostled." Jesus replied, "Yes, but I felt power surge through me. Someone touched me to be healed, and they received their healing." When the woman realized she couldn't hide any longer, she came and fell trembling at Jesus' feet. Before the entire crowd she declared, "I was desperate to touch you, Jesus, for I knew if I could just touch even the fringe of your garment I would be healed." Jesus responded, "Beloved daughter, your faith in me released your healing. You may go with my peace." (Luke 8:43-48 TPT)

Chapter 13

Quiet, Please.

I can't take any more noise.
I need to hear from my King.

That's where I've found myself lately - my soul is tired, my ears are ringing from too many voices, opinions, sermons, noise. Some good. Some not. But all of it is too much.

I can't sift through it anymore.
I don't want the sound of it anymore.
I want the whisper of my King.

Sometimes the most powerful thing I can say is no.
No to the over-talking.
No to the analyzing.
No to the uninvited advice.
No to the people who think they know what I need better than I do.
Even better than God does.

I don't need a checklist.
I don't need another conference.
I don't need a podcast, another "word", a platform, or a plan.

I need Him.

The One who knows how to breathe peace over chaos.
The One who can still the shaking in my chest and the ache in my core.
The One who was with me in the dark, when no one else showed up.
The One who held my heart when I couldn't even find it myself.

I've said yes to too much.
I've handed out pieces of me to people who didn't handle them with care.
I've let others speak louder than the Spirit.

But I'm reclaiming my stillness.
I'm pulling the curtain closed.
I'm turning the volume down.
Because I need to hear from my King.

This is a sacred place.
This is the hush of holy ground, a holy hush.
This is where healing happens.

So I say again—

Quiet, please.

I'm not being dramatic.
I'm not being distant.
I'm being committed.

I'm leaning in to the One Whose voice doesn't wound me.
I'm making room for the Whisper that restores me.
I'm shutting out the crowd to welcome Jesus.

Because there are things He wants to say to me that I can't afford to miss.
He has words for the broken part of me—words that don't rush, don't shame, don't pressure, and don't condemn.

Just truth.
Just love.
Just presence.

Let the world chatter. Let them misunderstand. I no longer care.
I'm not here for them.
I'm here for Him.

Activation

Find a quiet place today. Literally or spiritually.
Put your phone down. Close the door. Turn the worship music off.
Sit in the silence.

Feel the silence, even if it aches.

Ask this simple question:

"Jesus, is there anything You want to say to me today?"

Then listen.

If you can, write down what you hear. If you hear nothing, just sit.

Trust that, even in silence, He is with you.

Even silence can be holy.

Prayer

Jesus, quiet the noise.
Help me tune in to the sound of Your voice.
Remove the voices that confuse me, rush me, and shame me.
Make me sensitive again to Your whispers.
I only want what comes from You.
Amen.

Chapter 14

Through It All

I have found that I have spent most of my life trying to trust an unseen God.

I've spent my entire adult life learning about His character—

who He is, and who He is in my life...

Through my ignorance.

Through my brokenness.

Through my fears.

Through my insecurities.

Through my prodigal journey.

Through my religious phase.

Through my angry phase.

Through my healing.

Through changes in my body.

Through learning about myself.

Through all of my failures.

Through physical pain.

Through mental torment.

Through every loss.

Through every demonic attack.

Through every doubt.

Through every betrayal.

Through all of the weeping.

Through all of the questioning.

God has not once changed His mind about me.

He has never stopped looking at me.

He has never once been ashamed of me.

He has never lashed out at me in anger.

All my life—even before I knew Him—He was good to me.

He loves every part of me.

That is so amazing to me.

That someone can love me like that… while knowing everything about me.

Through it all—

Past. Present. Future.

His love changed everything for me and about me.

All my life, I questioned my life's meaning and purpose.

All my life, I struggled to understand holiness and perfect love in God.

All my life, I searched for something—anything—tangible that I could hold on to.

Something I could control.

But I've learned: that's not how this works.

All I have is my testimony.

What He's done.

At first, it was an excitement. A newness.

Then I quickly learned that I couldn't do it.

I couldn't earn His love.

And I felt like such a failure.

I decided that church wasn't for me.

So I left.

But God did not leave me.

I was still His girl.

And He chased me for seven years.

Seven years.

He chased me until I was sick for His love.

Until I ached for Him.

Until I turned around, ran into His arms, and melted into Him.

This is my foundation:

He never left me.

This is the way out.

Activation

Take some time this week and ask yourself:

Where has God chased me and I didn't even see it?

What lies have I believed about His love?

Have I been trying to earn something that was always meant to be a gift?

Write your own "Through it all" list—just like the one above.

Name the seasons you've walked through.

Then speak over it: He never left me. Not once.

Prayer

God,

You never gave up on me. Not once.

Even when I ran, even when I doubted, even when I didn't trust You—You stayed.

Thank You for loving me through all of it.

Thank You for chasing me until I was ready to be found.

Thank You for never changing Your mind about me.

Let this love be my foundation.

Let this truth be my way out.

In Jesus' name,

Amen.

Chapter 15

The Furnace

When My Heart Woke Up

This morning, I was thinking about the darkest time in my life.
And surprisingly, it wasn't the abuse.
It wasn't the domestic violence.
It wasn't the stuff in between.

It was the healing. The actual healing process.

That's when I wanted to die. That's when I asked God to kill me.

I was filled with rage. Venom. Bitterness. I was walking through my own dark night of the soul.

I was so entangled with pain that I couldn't see the way out. I didn't see a future. Hope was gone. I had nothing left to hold onto—but what I had been holding onto was shallow anyway.

Work.
False hopes.
Shallow dreams.

I didn't know how to dream. I didn't know how to live beyond survival. I didn't know how to pursue anything meaningful. And then God said something that shook the ground I was standing on.

He said, Enough!

And He took my hand. I didn't want to go, but He led me back…
Back to where it all started.

Not just to the memories I remembered. He took me to the ones I had forgotten. The ones buried so deep I didn't know they were there.

And that's when I truly wanted to die.

That was my furnace. My fire. It was painful.

But He was there. All the way through it, He never left me.

There were moments when I could hear Him weeping with me. There was one moment in particular I'll never forget. I heard Him say: "I will take the blame for everything that happened."

And just like that, I saw the Cross. I saw all that He became so I could be free. And not just me—but even the ones who had abused me. I realized then—I had no right to keep holding onto unforgiveness.

I had to let go of the bitterness. I had to choose the harder way: forgiveness.

And when I did, everything began to change. Things started breaking off of me—one by one. Layers peeled back. Chains fell. The prison door swung open.

But it wasn't something that happened quick. It was a process. And I had a part to play.

I had to say: Yes, I'm willing. Even when it hurt. Even when it felt unbearable.

But I was never alone.

And it was hard. But it was worth it.

I no longer skim the surface of life. I live with depth now. I love with depth.

Because now—I know what love is. And I know how to love others. It's worth it. Your freedom is worth it.

I've walked with Jesus through some of the deepest, most intimate places—and I wouldn't trade any of it. Not a single flame in the furnace. Not a single tear.

All of your healing is available. Every ounce of it.

Jesus gave every drop of His blood for your freedom. So go get it. Go after every bit of healing that's yours.

You don't have to walk alone. Find someone to link arms with. You were never meant to do this alone. Go after every ounce of your freedom.

Activation

Take a moment today and sit with this question:

What are you still holding onto that Jesus already paid for?

Is it rage?
Bitterness?
Fear?
Control?

Write it down. Be honest.

Then ask the Holy Spirit to show you what it looks like to surrender it—fully.

Reach out to someone who can walk with you. This healing journey was never meant to be done in isolation. Let someone in.

Prayer

Jesus,
I want all the healing You died to give me.
Even the parts I'm afraid to touch.
Even the memories I buried.
Even the places that still ache.

I say yes today.
Yes to walking with You into the pain.
Yes to letting go of what's kept me stuck.
Yes to freedom.

Thank You for never leaving me.
Thank You for weeping with me.
Thank You for taking the blame—so I could be free.

Help me walk with You, step by step,
Until every ounce of my heart is fully alive again.

In Your name,
Amen.

Chapter 16

My Body, His Temple.

My body is not my enemy.

More often than not, people who have been sexually abused often grow up with a negative view of themselves, even loathing their bodies.

When we are violated as a child, we often struggle with where our bodies begin and where they end. In other words, we don't understand boundaries because they have already been violated. Your "NO" was not validated. Your personal space was non-existent.

Let's talk about this.

This can mean so many things for you as an adult.

You continue to get walked on and taken advantage of because you have not learned a healthy "NO".

You continue to get involved with people who abuse you. There are so many forms of abuse.

Spiritual abuse - manipulation, controlling, shaming, using scripture to control you or excuse their abusive behavior.

Sexual abuse - ritualistic, physical, visual.

Verbal abuse - screaming and shouting to hurt you or cause you harm or to control you. Or, mocking you, calling you names and using derogatory language about you.

Physical abuse - hitting, kicking, pinching, shaking, throwing things at you, etc.

Abuse can be from a parent, aunt, uncle, sibling, any authority figure, a spouse, boyfriend, girlfriend . . . .

It is NEVER ok and if you are being abused right now while reading this book - get help! Get away and get help!

Jesus wants to restore your body image and your relationship with your body.

That's right, restore your relationship with your body.

But before reconciliation can begin with your body, you have to first acknowledge that you were wronged. You might even feel that your body betrayed you. I did!

But your body didn't betray you, your abuser did.

This could have a profound effect on both men and women who have experienced abuse, where their physical body was a weapon and they came to believe it was a source of pain, even their enemy. All kinds of body image distortion (people who are overweight, abused, loathing their body or "at war" with their own physical body) need to be healed.

Let's start by acknowledging that your body has been the source of heartache, emotion and spiritual pain. Maybe you were made fun of when you were younger. Maybe a certain body part was criticized.

Are you at war with your body or are you at peace with your body?

I feel convicted right now. I think we need to ask our body to forgive us and allow healing to come.

Start here - (insert your name), will you forgive me for being so hard on you over the years? Forgive me for the harm that I have caused you, loathing you, rejecting and abandoning you, betraying you. Forgive me for neglecting you,

I declare my body to be a blessing and not a curse. My body is God's beautiful and precious temple!

Remove yourself from being in war with your body. Your body is a blessing to the Lord. Receive this and believe this for yourself.

Activation

I am loved.

I am blessed.
My body is His temple.
My body is not my enemy and I am not my body's enemy.

Start at the top of your body and work your way down to the soles of your feet, blessing and repenting as you feel led.

I bless my mind. Move down to your feet .. blessing each part . . legs, arms, heart, eyes . . all of YOU!

Here are a few Bible verses for you to start with.

… 'for, "Who has known the mind of the Lord
so as to instruct him?" But we have the mind of Christ.' (1 Corinthians 2:16 NIV)

"Therefore, I urge you, brothers and sisters, in view of God's mercy, to offer your bodies as a living sacrifice, holy and pleasing to God—this is your true and proper worship. Do not conform to the pattern of this world, but be transformed by the renewing of your mind. Then you will be able to test and approve what God's will is—his good, pleasing and perfect will." (Romans 12:1-2 NIV)

"The words of the reckless pierce like swords, but the tongue of the wise brings healing." (Proverbs 12:18 NIV)

'Jesus replied: '"Love the Lord your God with all your heart and with all your soul and with all your mind." This is the first and greatest commandment. And the second is like it: "Love your neighbor as yourself."' (Matthew 22: 37-39 NIV)

Speaking God's Word over my life is what has brought true transformation and healing to me. It is powerful and living. We can not truly be healed without it.

Prayer

Lord, Bless my body.

Forgive me Lord for not loving myself. Your word tells me to love my friends the way that I love myself. How can I really love until I learn to love me? I bless me, my body. Teach me Your ways, Your precepts and to really love and value the person that You made me to be.

Bless you friend! In Jesus' Mighty Name!

Chapter 17

Heal My Vision

Fragmented Vision… Whole Eyes.

Think about this for a second: if you are fragmented in your soul, that means you are not whole. Fragmentation comes from hurt - deep trauma, wounds that haven't fully healed. And when your soul is fragmented, you're likely seeing the world through that brokenness.

You're not seeing through ***wholeness***.

When we see the world through a healed, whole lens, we begin to look at life with soft eyes - eyes that can see things as they truly are.

But when you're viewing life through a fragmented soul, you're filtering everything through shattered pieces of pain. Your heart may still be in a million tiny pieces, and that brokenness shows up everywhere: in your emotions, your personality, your perspective, your words.

You don't see life *clearly*. You see it through the *cracks*.

So what does it look like to see with ***whole eyes***?

What does it look like to live with whole, healthy vision?

Let me give you a picture:

I often use furniture as an example because it helps me connect the invisible to the visible.

Imagine a chair.

If I have soft eyes—eyes formed through healing and wholeness—I'm able to sit back and take in the full picture. I can admire its beauty, but I'm also able to notice the flaws: a cracked leg, a wobbly base, something that needs repair.

I'll sit carefully, or maybe I won't sit at all.

Why?

Because I see it for what it actually is. That's "soft vision".

But if I have fragmented vision, if I'm still looking through hard eyes—through trauma, hypervigilance, or fear—I'm only going to see what I want to see.

Maybe the chair is beautiful on the outside, and that's all I choose to focus on. I miss the warning signs. I sit down expecting it to hold me, and it collapses. This is what happens when we ignore the full truth because our lens is still cracked.

Soft eyes see the whole picture.

Hard eyes see very limited.

This is the difference between healed vision and fractured sight.

The other part of having fragmented sight is that I was still broken and hypervigilant, I saw danger in everything. I expected to be hurt, abandoned, rejected, or violated. So I looked for it. I was constantly on alert. That's how trauma programs us to survive—but it doesn't allow us to thrive.

Even after the past remained the same, the way I saw life began to shift as healing took place. I'm no longer living in constant alert mode. And when those old patterns try to rise up, I now have the tools to stop and ask myself:

"Is this real, or is this a trigger?"

Sometimes, I take a step back. I remove myself from the situation entirely. Other times, I breathe deep, sit still, and remember:

This isn't that.

This moment is not my past. I'm safe now.

Healing allows you to see clearly. It doesn't change what happened. It changes how you see. It gives you back soft eyes, whole eyes—eyes that can finally rest.

Activation

Practice Soft Vision

1. Check your lens.

Reflect on how you're seeing a current situation. Are you responding through old wounds or present reality?

2. Breathe and ask:

Is this a trigger or truth?

Am I seeing the full picture, or just a sliver of it?

3. Practice pause.

Next time you feel yourself tense up or brace for harm, pause and ask Jesus to help you see with soft eyes. Wholeness sees more clearly than fear ever could.

4. Speak this out loud:

"I am not my past. I see with whole eyes. I live from a healed heart."

Prayer

Jesus,

You are the restorer of broken things. You see every piece of my shattered soul, and You hold them gently. Teach me what it means to see with soft eyes—eyes that don't flinch, eyes that don't panic, eyes that see beauty, flaws, and truth all at once.

When I still feel fragmented, I pray for wholeness. I pray for peace. I ask You to begin the deep work of healing the places that are still raw. Help me live from a healed heart, not a wounded one.

Thank You for being the One who sees clearly and still loves fully.

I receive Your eyes today.

Amen.

Chapter 18

Redeeming Nightmares

Have you ever had a dream that was so real and so scary?

This particular one I am recalling was absolutely terrifying.

I looked around and realized that it was around 2 or 3 in the morning. I woke up in a full-blown panic. It happened again and again and the next thing I knew, years had gone by.

I was tormented, thinking, "why am I having the same recurring nightmare?"

This happened to me for years, until I learned that I can take control of my sleep by surrendering my dreams to my sweet Jesus.

Not only were my nightmares resolved, my dreams began to be filled with hope, wonder and redemption because Jesus began to author and redeem my dreams.

I surrendered my dreams and my sleep to the Lord.

My simple prayer was, "Lord, you be the Lord of my sleep!"

When I got that, I began to heal, and deep, deep healing is what I needed.

I needed my spirit to be healed and I needed my physical body to be healed from the trauma, from the memory that I was carrying in my body.

Before this, my dreams were intense and terrifying for years.

I don't know if you remember in the earlier part of the book, but I talked about domestic violence. I was only 17 when it started.

Fast forward, I had just turned 20 and I needed to get away from my abusive home. I needed to be "safe". I needed to take control of my life somehow and my solution would be by getting married to someone else.

My dominant thought was, "If that is what I needed and what was going to have to happen to give me some control and safety in my life, then that's what I'll do."

Regretfully, that's what I did.

And to me, looking back, it wasn't a true marriage in honor of my amazing husband of more than twenty years now.

I talk very little about what happened to me but I think it's important that I share with you inside of the cover of this book.

Before I married the wrong guy…I was in a very serious situation. He was a very wicked man. After severe emotional and verbal abuse, thinking it could not get worse, it did.

There were times when I thought that I would surely die. This is what led me to the decision to run. I ran and I ran.

I finally left and I hid from him, but he found me everywhere I went. He was a very narcissistic person and he was able to turn everything around to make me feel like a bad person.

Fast forward to the escape. After a couple of years of increased abuse, I left.

The nightmares began kicking in and they didn't stop even after I became born again. I did get a new hope. I felt like I had a new lease on life but nighttime was hard. Night time was scary. I dreaded sleep because everything that had ever happened to me was locked up inside. The nightmares released the monsters.

Years later, even after I found out that this individual died, I would dream that he would come back to life, find me and kill me.

For many years, he was abusive to me in my dreams, but looking back, I realize that those were demonic dreams. It wasn't actually him coming back, coming into my dreams. One after another, more nightmares recurred about how I was abused . .

Aaron, my amazing husband of over 21 years now, and my partner in true healing, told me that the nightmares increased because I had stepped into healing.

I had stepped into my healing journey and things would get harder before they got better.

A dear friend of mine told me to just begin to surrender my dream life to Jesus and so I did. I began to surrender my dreams to Jesus and this is what it looked like. I sat on the edge of my bed (and sometimes I still do it) and talked to Jesus.

With outstretched hands, I surrendered my dreams to Jesus. I asked Him to come and be the Lord of my dreams, to be the Lord of my sleep, and be the Lord of my emotions. Also, I asked Him to be the Lord of my spirit. I invited him to become the Lord of me as I slept. When I layed down, I became vulnerable and I needed him to Shepherd me.

I need Jesus to Shepherd me and to Shepherd my spirit and be the Lord of my sleep. I needed Jesus to be the Lord of my dreams so that the enemy cannot come in and manipulate me and assault me spiritually while my body was sleeping.

We are very vulnerable when we sleep and we need Jesus to protect us. I'm going to walk you through this activation. I'm going to give you some verses of scripture to chew on. It's very important for your healing journey that you soak in the scriptures.

We will also want to talk about the music you're listening to, the movies you are watching and the books that you're reading.

This is not about religion or the rules.

The Bible says, everything is permissible but not everything is beneficial.

You are especially vulnerable, now, when you're wide open in the healing process. When you begin to "let Him", your heart becomes more tender for the first time in a long time. And, you don't have any "skin" over your heart. Because of this, it is so important to be careful what you're watching, what you're listening to, and who you surround yourself with.

It's important to listen. It's important for you to understand what you're listening to. You can talk to Jesus about that later. Right now I want you to just begin to surrender your dreams.

Activation

Soak in soaking worship music before bed.

Lift your precious hands to Jesus and surrender your sleep and your dreams to Him. Ask Him to redeem the nightmares. Ask Him to take you into the green pasture that is just for you and Him. Wait on the edge of your bed until you feel that sweet release, His peace.

Do this over and over until one day, the nightmares cease.

Read the Word of God over yourself.

Ask for prayer.

Scripture reading for healing your dreams:

"Lord, hide Your word in me so that I won't fall into sin." (Psalm 119:11 TPT)

"The Lord is my shepherd, I lack nothing. He makes me lie down in green pastures, he leads me beside quiet waters, he refreshes my soul.

He guides me along the right paths for his name's sake. Even though I walk through the darkest valley, I will fear no evil, for you are with me; your rod and your staff, they comfort me.

You prepare a table before me in the presence of my enemies. You anoint my head with oil; my cup overflows.

"Surely your goodness and love will follow me all the days of my life, and I will dwell in the house of the Lord forever." (Psalm 23 NIV)

Prayer

Jesus, thank you that You never leave me. Thank you for redeeming my dreams and my imagination. You are my Shepherd and I lack nothing. You make me lie down in green pastures. You lead me beside still waters and you refresh my soul. You guide me along the right paths for your name's sake! You comfort me and prepare a table for me in the presence of my enemies. Your goodness and your love will follow me all the days of my life. I will dwell in Your house forever!

Thank Him and speak these gems over yourself every night.

Be free, darling!

Chapter 19

Be, Just Be

There was a time I couldn't sit still - not just in my body, but in my soul.

Being still felt unsafe.

Silence was loud.

And rest? Rest felt like laziness or worse - vulnerability.

I had learned early in life that being still meant I could be caught. Hurt. Touched in ways a child never should be. My body remembered what my mind tried to forget. And so I stayed busy.

Always moving and always proving.

I thought if I could just do more, be more, achieve more, I could outrun the ache I carried in my chest. But the ache was never behind me. It was always inside me.

I didn't know how to "be."

I only knew how to survive.

I had read the verse so many times:

"Surrender your anxiety. Be still and realize that I am God. I am God above all the nations, and I am exalted throughout the whole earth." (Psalms 46:10 TPT)

I used to skim past it, not because I didn't believe it, but because I didn't know how to live it.

Be still?

How?

I didn't even know who I was when I wasn't performing, fixing or helping someone else. I confused busyness with purpose and exhaustion with holiness. But eventually, the weight of all that "doing" broke me.

And in the breaking, I heard a whisper:

"You don't have to strive to be loved. You already are. You don't have to strive to be healed. Just be with Me."

It wasn't overnight. Healing never is. But slowly, like rivers smoothing jagged rocks, I learned to let go. I started to lean back.

I began to trust the current of grace.

One morning, while sitting on the front porch, holding my little girl on my lap with our faces against the wind, I felt it for the first time: ***peace***.

Not because the trauma had disappeared. Not because everything was perfect, but because I had stopped fighting the river—and started letting it carry me.

Jesus didn't just invite me to follow Him. He invited me to abide.

All I could hear was this whisper: Let Him. Let the Healer heal you.

"Are you weary, carrying a heavy burden? Come to me. I will refresh your life, for I am your oasis." (Matthew 11:28 TPT)

I was so weary.

But rest was waiting for me—not on the other side of doing everything right, but in the simple, sacred act of just being with Him.

Activation

Let the Rivers Carry You

This is a sacred moment. You don't have to perform here. You don't have to be strong. Just be.

Find a quiet place where you can sit or lie down without interruption. Place your hand over your heart. Close your eyes. Take three deep breaths.

As you breathe, picture yourself on a front porch. You are holding the little girl, that you once were, on your lap. Her face is pressed against the wind. She is safe.

She is seen. She is held. Let this be your beginning place.

Step 1: Acknowledge

Whisper this aloud:

> "Jesus, I've been so tired from trying to hold it all together. I don't always know how to rest, but I want to learn."

Write in your journal:

What have I been carrying that I was never meant to carry?
Where do I feel the pressure to prove or perform in order to feel worthy?

Step 2: Release

Open your hands as a physical sign of surrender. Pray:

> "Lord, I give You my need to be strong. I lay down the striving. I lay down the fear that I won't be enough if I stop moving."

Then write:

What would it feel like to trust Jesus enough to simply be?
What am I afraid will happen if I stop striving?

Step 3: Receive

Now imagine Jesus sitting beside you. Feel His nearness, not rushing you, not expecting anything—just being with you.

Write this in your journal and speak it aloud:

> "Jesus, teach me how to rest. I want to be still and know You. I want to trust the river of Your love to carry me."

Then answer:

When was the last time I felt peace? What did it feel like in my body, in my soul?
What is one small way I can practice 'just being' this week—without guilt or pressure?

Prayer

Jesus, You are not asking me to perform.
You are not measuring me by my productivity.
You are inviting me to come close—to abide, to rest, to simply be.
Help me to lay down the armor I've carried for too long.
Teach me how to trust again.
Be my shelter, my river, my rest.
I give You permission to carry me.
I am Yours.

Amen

SECTION THREE: Transformation & Identity

After the digging comes the becoming. Here, you'll begin to rediscover who you are beyond abuse, rejection, and fear. These chapters help you rebuild your voice, your trust, and your God-given identity - piece by piece.

Chapter 20

Forgiveness

What a day!

I'll never forget the day that I decided to be free! It was the day that I forgave the man that abused me. I'd like to tell you about it.

All my life I carried a bitterness of soul. It ran deep. I wanted acknowledgement of what had been done. I wanted someone to pay. I wanted the bitterness to no longer taunt me. I wanted to be set free from the nightmares.

I was born again at the age of 21. I was filled with zeal and passion for Christ. But I was still very wounded and broken. I couldn't escape the shame and the torment that cloaked me. Every time I looked in the mirror, I saw someone that I hated. I wanted to die. I begged God to take my life.

Why did I have to go through this? Why couldn't my abuser just come forward and say how sorry he was and beg for forgiveness? Why did I have to forgive him? He almost destroyed my life.

I was newly married and so broken. If you are reading this and you are in that place . . . there's hope. Keep reading.

Aaron and I were talking in our bedroom one day. I was filled with rage. I was filled with disgust and bitterness of soul. I was weeping. My husband was just listening and so attentive.

He was sitting on the bed and I was standing at the foot of the bed. I yelled desperately, "who will pay for this?' I remember thinking that somehow it would ease my pain!

Jesus.

Immediately after me asking that question in the fit of rage . . . I saw Jesus. He stood right in the middle of that room, raised His hand and said . . . "I will."

I wept. I broke. I fell on my face and knew that I no longer had an excuse to hold any unforgiveness towards my abuser. This was the beginning of my beautiful and messy journey towards wholeness and why I am writing this book. ***It's the way out.***

It's the arrow that points to the way out.

I acknowledged what happened. I owned my pain. I accepted the fact that Jesus, my best friend, became my abuser on the cross. He didn't just hang on that cross. He became the child abuser, the sinner that molested me as a child and a teenager. He became all of that so that he could set my abuser free! I knew right then that He loved them, too. And I had no right to not forgive.

I let go of my "rights" that day. I let go of any entitlement that I carried and let go of that right to continue to be a victim. This was the beginning of my forgiveness journey and I am still walking that out.

I asked Jesus to help me. I know that I was not able to do this without His grace and wisdom. And He helped me. I walked it out every single day. I spoke scripture out loud. I asked God for help, outloud. I processed with my husband. I held onto what I knew to be good and true and decided that I wanted God to do whatever it would take to help me, to set me free. I gave God permission to do whatever it would take.

About a year later I received visitors. They came for a visit and little did I know that this was a setup by the Holy Spirit. We were visiting when my abuser offered to take the trash out for me. I agreed.

I felt it was time.

I walked outside and saw him walking back towards the house. I walked towards him and decided to confront him. I didn't think much about what would happen next.

We met in the backyard face to face. I looked up at his broken face and told him that what he had done to me was wrong. I told him that he almost destroyed my life but because of Jesus, he did not.

In that moment I saw a grown man melt and weep and repent. There was so much sorrow and so much emotion. He asked me if I could ever forgive him. I did. I told him that I forgive him as Christ had forgiven me.

All of a sudden I felt this weight lift off of me. I felt so light and it was all gone. I knew that what had happened to me was no longer who I am, and it was just something that happened to me.

My abuse was no longer my identity.

After that day, I have been able to talk about what happened without feeling the shame and feeling so tainted. I knew that I had been set free that day. And so did he.

This man that did these terrible things to me repented and became a free man. He has since passed away and is now with Jesus. I watched God do miracles in his life and in my own life because of that single act of forgiveness.

I see unforgiveness as a black and powerful rope that binds us to God's enemy. I see it as something that blinds us and keeps our hearts bound up in sin.

I was only able to forgive by faith at first.

Everyday I walked it out by faith… everyday until one day it wasn't an effort. Since then, I have had to heal a lot. I have had to walk out my own salvation with fear and trembling. I have needed to own my own garbage and repent. I needed to change!

I realized that I can't blame everything, or actually, anything on what happened to me. I was set free and there came a time for me to step out of the blame and the victim mentality.

I let Him!

I want to pray for you that God will show you where you are still bound up and in sin. I want to ask Jesus to help you to let go and completely forgive. He may not do it the way that He did it for me. Your abuser(s) may not be available, willing or even alive, but Jesus can work miracles in your life and heart if you let Him. You may never have the opportunity to reconcile, but with God, you can get 100% free through forgiveness. Your story with Jesus is your very own story with Jesus. It's special and unique. And soon you will have your own testimony!

Pray this prayer with me.

Jesus, help me. I'm angry and I hurt. I need you to help me. I give you permission to do whatever it takes to get me to the place where you want me to be. Help me to trust You where I don't trust You. Help my unbelief.

Has God graciously forgiven you? (read Ephesians 4:32 TPT)

Forgive me as I release those who've wronged me. (read Matthew 6:12 TPT)

Activation

Take your time. Please understand the depth of your pain. Don't let others dictate to you anything outside of God's beautiful counsel. This is important and a crucial part of your healing.

Acknowledge that what happened to you was not your fault.

Acknowledge that it was wrong.

Acknowledge that what happened to you caused your soul to be deeply wounded and it will take time to heal, even after forgiveness.

Don't share this with just anyone. Keep your pearls close to your heart - Matthew 7:6.

Choose, by faith, to let Him. Let Jesus help you in the area of forgiveness. Journal it. Walk this out with Him. Let Him tell you the hard truth.

It's worth it! It is so hard at first but it is vital to your soul health. Without forgiveness we can not receive all that God has for us. The scripture says when we forgive, we are forgiven.

I look at my life now with all of its blessings and the freedom that I carry and know that it was birthed from that one single act of choosing to forgive.

May the Lord bless you as you walk this out and give you the grace to forgive those who've hurt you in the most heinous ways.

Chapter 21

Reconciliation

At the cross.

This is where we deal with that reconciliation that we have a hard time grasping.

Be reconciled to God through Christ Jesus, at the cross.

I want to give you something to chew on for a while.

God. Really. Really. Loves. You.

When we reconcile to God, everything else comes after.

"Seek the Kingdom of God above all else, and live righteously, and he will give you everything you need." (Matthew 6:33 NLT)

That makes more sense to me now than it ever has before. If you want a greater understanding of why we are reconciled to some and not to others . . . go there.

We need to understand things in a deeper way so that we can move past our hurts and move into wholeness. I will get into that in my next book.

I searched online for the definition of "reconcile" and hope that it encourages you.

rec·on·cile means:

restore friendly relations between.
"she wanted to be reconciled with her father"
cause to coexist in harmony; make or show to be compatible.

Similar concepts:
make compatible
harmonize
make harmonious

cause to be in agreement
adjust
balance
attune

What a beautiful, glorious and spectacular miracle…that we can be reconciled to God!

We can also be reconciled to ourselves and to others!

We can only be reconciled to God through the blood of His Son, Jesus and that is by accepting the work that He did on the cross and repenting. Just turn around and reject everything that is not from Jesus!! Turn to the east and receive all that He has for you and accept the work that Jesus did, all of it. And be reconciled to your Father.

That will bring harmony to your soul and then you can really begin to heal and love yourself.

I want to walk through something with you and I hope it will help you with some long overdue closure regarding relationships that have tormented and confused you.

Forgiveness.

You have to forgive so that you can begin the process of reconciliation with your abuser. They may never acknowledge the pain that they've caused you.

This is something that I am still walking through. I was able to walk through much of it, and it was so hard.

I have never had a deep relationship with my mother. There are still a lot of unspoken things that impact our relationship in a very negative way. She just doesn't want to talk about it. She doesn't want to revisit places that are too painful for her. And that means that she is unwilling to go there with me and be reconciled.

As I write this, I understand, I think. Her story is not mine and she may tell you something very different. In fact, I know that she would because she has her own story and her own journey to walk out.

I am learning to release the negative memories and all of the negative words so that I can be reconciled. I may never be reconciled to her, but I can choose to forgive her, daily.

Everyone that has ever hurt me will have to deal with that one way or another. I want to choose forgiveness now. I know that there is freedom in that. I know that Christ became my sin and died as me on that cross so that I can walk in complete freedom. I know that He did the same for you.

Listen beloved - We cannot be reconciled to everyone who has ever hurt us or that we have ever hurt. Both parties have to be willing. I am learning that not everyone is willing. God knows that very well. He painfully knows that not everyone that He loves is willing to be reconciled to Him. It's there, He's willing, He wants it . . . but not everyone will.

We can still offer our love and forgiveness but at some point, we have to accept that it's time to let go and move on.

My abuser repented, acknowledged all that he had done and therefore reconciliation happened. See what I said there?

Repent, agree with God, be reconciled and be free to have a beautiful relationship!

When we are truly reconciled to God, we can really love those who have broken us and forgive them.

Dear Beloved,

I am sorry for all that has broken you. I am sorry that your heart sometimes feels like it is in a million little pieces. I know that Jesus wants to hold your heart and put all the pieces back together. I know that there is freedom just ahead for you.

I know that as you lay down the burdens, the bitterness and unforgiveness . . . you'll begin to fly.

Your heart will soar like an eagle. You will learn to smile and play and dance. You will no longer have those nightmares. You will encounter God in ways that you never thought possible. All because you reconciled to Abba.

Love will absolutely melt you. You will no longer be falling apart. You will come to life. You will no longer have the triggers that you've always had. You will find your voice and begin your own journey with Jesus by helping others, just like you, to become free!

Activation

Go back to the Cross and sit with Christ there for a while. Bring your journal and your Bible. Feel free to listen to some soaking music or just sit in the quiet.

Ask Jesus to guide you beyond the Cross.

Ask Jesus to help you become reconciled to Abba.

Be willing to move into beautiful encounters through dreams and visions. God may even begin to speak to you through people about your identity. Write it all down. Ask God to give you life scriptures and hold on tight to all of them.

Save every word.

Beloved, Jesus loves you. Abba loves you. Holy Spirit loves you. I love you.

Be free. Be reconciled.

Prayer

Just thank Him.

Thank Him for all that He has done.

Do you eat? Thank Him.
Do you have shelter? Thank Him.
Do you have clothing on your back? Thank Him?
Are you breathing? Thank Him.

Just sit with Him and thank Him.

Scripture: Matthew 6:33, Colossians 1:20, 1 Timothy 2:5, 2 Corinthians 5:18, 2 Corinthians 5:19, Ephesians 2:16, Colossians 1:22.

Be free!

Chapter 22

Be Free

Here's another tool in my mental health belt: baby and kid pictures of me!

You might find this very healing and helpful too.

That's right! I married those pictures with Romans 12:1-2 during a very difficult season of healing.

I couldn't look at myself because I hated who I saw in the mirror. I hated how I felt, the shame, guilt and how tainted I thought I was. All I could see was a complete distortion… a blob of flesh with a face.

I always talked down to the girl in the mirror. I told her that I hated her and I wanted her to die. I asked God multiple times to kill her. Living with her was tormenting and I was disgusted with her daily.

Someone gave me this tool 20 years ago and it has been the sharpest tool in my belt. I pulled out as many baby pictures and little girl pictures as I could find. I pinned them to a cork board. I put the board in a place where I could see it easily.

I memorized Romans 12:1-2 and began speaking it over the girl in the mirror daily. I forced myself to look at her until finally…..

I no longer hated her and no longer cursed her. I broke every curse that I spoke and that others spoke over me. I began to look for things that I liked about me. And every time I was tempted to curse her, I'd look at that little girl on the cork board. There's no way I could speak to her that way!

Those pictures stayed out for a few years. After some significant healing in my heart toward myself, I finally put them away. Also, God gave me 2 more little daughters and through them, He began to heal me in other precious and miraculous ways. I told myself one day: you'll never talk to them the way you've talked to yourself but you're also done cursing yourself and that little girl in you!

It's not that we've forgotten our value, rather, we never knew our value. This is a personal and difficult journey. But it's the most important gift that you can give to yourself.

Let the scripture validate you. Remember to give Grace to yourself.. Everyone wants grace but so often we forget to give it to ourselves.

You're valuable. You're unique. You're solely yourself. You're loved with a powerful and intense love. We need you. You bring a spice to the table that no one else can.

Let God's word transform you right beside His love. Look for those sweet little pictures of you and put them out. When you are tempted to criticize your face, hips, voice, intelligence, heart, gifts… don't.

I triple dog dare you to speak horrible words over those sweet little kid pictures of you. YOU CAN'T!

Activation

Get a small cork board and some tacks or tape. Find as many baby and childhood photos of yourself as you can, and pin them to the board. Place it somewhere you'll see often. Look at that baby—bless her with Scripture. It's okay if you don't feel it. Do it anyway.

Lord, I offer up to you my body as a living sacrifice . . may it be holy and pleasing to you.

Pray this over the mirror while you look yourself in the eyes. Stay there for a while. Come back tomorrow, stay. Pray. Stay.

Suddenly you will no longer loathe yourself.

"Jesus said to the people who believed in him, "You are truly my disciples if you remain faithful to my teachings. And you will know the truth, and the truth will set you free." (John 8: 31 & 32 NLT)

"So Christ has truly set us free. Now make sure that you stay free, and don't get tied up again in slavery to the law." (Galatians 5:1 NLT)

"For you have been called to live in freedom, my brothers and sisters. But don't use your freedom to satisfy your sinful nature. Instead, use your freedom to serve one another in love." (Galatians 5:13 NLT)

"But now you are free from the power of sin and have become slaves of God. Now you do those things that lead to holiness and result in eternal life." (Romans 6:22 NLT)

"So if the Son sets you free, you are truly free." (John 8:36 NLT)

Christ did not just release freedom over you for the sake of just being free. Free to live and dance and love! He wants you to be free from the law, free from sin. Free to love without reserve! I promise you . . . it's coming for you!

Chapter 23

Self-Talk

When I talk to myself this is normally what I say. Oh my soul, what's your worry oh my soul? What's your hurry? Oh my soul, look to the hills where your help comes from. Oh my soul, why are you so downcast within me?

It's in moments like this when I can encourage myself but also allow myself to go through what I'm going through and even feel what I feel.

But I think it's important to remind our souls that our feelings are not always telling us the truth. This is why I talk to myself.

I talk to myself to say things like:

"You are his beloved."

"He gets excited about you."

"You are a daughter of the most high God."

"You are forgiven."

"You have been redeemed."

"You've been restored."

"You are being renewed."

"You are a loved and highly favored daughter."

I've been on my healing journey for more than 20 years now and it does get easier but I'm still on it. I think that I will always be on my healing journey until I see Jesus face-to-face.

I face new challenges all the time but they are no longer the challenges that I used to face. I am an overcomer, I am a fighter, I am a front runner, I really do have a very strong spirit and I believe that this is why I've survived all the things that I have endured.

I like to say that I'm spicy.

What's your unique spice?

Remembering when I was a little girl I would talk to myself and encourage myself that it would be over soon. I would encourage myself as a child, saying to myself, "it won't always be this way… this will be over soon."

And then one day I no longer had to say that to myself because it was over. And now, just like you, I work through the side effects of childhood sexual abuse. It isn't easy.

It isn't easy to learn to trust. It isn't easy to feel good in your soul about who you are. It's a fight. This is why I believe that reading scripture over yourself is so very important. That's where my healing began.

There was a time where I couldn't look at myself in the mirror because I hated myself. So I took it step-by-step, tiny little steps. I began to read scripture over myself and make myself stay in the mirror to look at the girl looking back at me. And eventually it became easy to look at the girl in the mirror and I decided that I think I even love the girl in the mirror.

One of the things I want to encourage you to do is to soak yourself in scripture even if you're not feeling it. Find a version that you really love. One that really speaks to you. One that speaks to you in your language.

My favorite right now is the passion translation. There is just something so special about the passion translation and I love reading it out loud. For me, when I read the passion translation, I feel as if I'm walking in the cool of the day and suddenly I am Cinderella… and I'm not kidding you, it's as if the animals just start talking to me.

On second thought, scratch that.

You don't have to love just one version. Maybe you have a few so I just encourage you to dig in.

Ephesians is a really good place to start. I also love reading the Psalms of David.

I just feel like David and I have so much in common and I understand his tears, his pain, and the words that he poured onto pages. And I also understood the ambivalence of being called a man or a woman after God's own heart and yet how is that even possible after all that I've done.

I get it.

But, the truth is that I am His beloved and the truth is that you are His beloved.

Find some of your favorite verses in the Bible. Write them down and add yourself to it, and then speak that to yourself every single day whether you believe it or not.

Speak it until you begin to believe it. There's something about speaking the Word out loud.

Faith comes by hearing but there's something about speaking the word of God over yourself. You hear it in your ears, and in your brain, but when you do it over and over and over, it lands and takes root in a good place inside of you.

It will eventually land in your soul, and the Holy Spirit will bring that back to you when you need it the most.

You will be reminded of a particular verse of Scripture that feeds you when you need it.

Do you remember the first Bible verse that you ever memorized? I do. I believe I was six or seven years old.

I grew up in a Southern Baptist church and so therefore I learned to speak scripture in the King James version.

The first Bible verse I remember being planted in my heart is, "Thy word have I hid in my heart that I might not sin against Thee." I think it's Psalm 119:11.

But it's amazing to me that it's the first verse of Scripture that I remember reading and reciting out loud, and here I am telling you to hide God's word in your heart. I believe it!

So, come with me into the mystical realm of God's word, until you start believing it. Speak it over and over and over and over.

Another one of my healing verses was Romans 12: 1-2 (NIV)...

"Therefore, I urge you, brothers and sisters, in view of God's mercy, to offer your bodies as a living sacrifice, holy and pleasing to God—this is your true and proper worship. 2 Do not conform to the pattern of this world, but be transformed by the renewing of your mind. Then you will be able to test and approve what God's will is—his good, pleasing and perfect will."

Activation

Take a moment now to look in the mirror. Breathe deeply. Say these words out loud with conviction, because they are true about you:

"I am His beloved."

"See what great love the Father has lavished on us, that we should be called children of God! And that is what we are! The reason the world does not know us is that it did not know him." (1 John 3:1 NIV)

"He gets excited about me."

"The Lord your God is with you, the Mighty Warrior who saves. He will take great delight in you; in his love he will no longer rebuke you, but will rejoice over you with singing." (Zephaniah 3:17 NIV)

"I am a daughter of the Most High God."

"But those who embraced him and took hold of his name he gave authority to become the children of God!" (John 1:12 TPT)

"I am forgiven."

"Since we are now joined to Christ, we have been given the treasures of redemption by his blood—the total cancellation of our sins—all because of the cascading riches of his grace." (Ephesians 1:7 TPT)

"I have been redeemed."

"Yet, Christ paid the full price to set us free from the curse of the law. He absorbed the curse completely as he became a curse in our place. For it is written: "Everyone who is hung upon a tree is cursed." (Galatians 3:13 TPT)

"I've been restored."

"That's where he restores and revives my life. He opens before me the right path and leads me along in his footsteps of righteousness so that I can bring honor to his name." (Psalms 23:3 TPT)

I've been made new.

"Now it's time to be made new by every revelation that's been given to you. (Ephesians 4:23 TPT)

I am accepted.

"And you did not receive the "spirit of religious duty," leading you back into the fear of never being good enough. But you have received the "Spirit of full acceptance," enfolding you into the family of God. And you will never feel orphaned, for as he rises up within us, our spirits join him in saying the words of tender affection, "Beloved Father!" (Romans 8:15 TPT)

Prayer

Jesus,

Help me speak to myself the way You speak to me—with truth, kindness, and grace.
When I'm tempted to be harsh or critical, remind me of who I am in You.
I am fearfully and wonderfully made.
I am loved, chosen, and never alone.
Let my thoughts line up with Your Word.
Let my words bring life, not shame.
Teach me to renew my mind and speak truth in love—to myself and others.
Today, I choose to believe what You say about me.

In Jesus' name,
Amen

Chapter 24

Self Care

Dearest darling,

I want to make sure that you understand the importance of self-care. Soul care, spirit care, body care . . . just care for yourself. I love you. You are loved. You are valuable.

I started with Romans 12:1-2 in The Passion Translation

"Beloved friends, what should be our proper response to God's marvelous mercies? I encourage you to surrender yourselves to God to be his sacred, living sacrifices. And live in holiness, experiencing all that delights his heart. For this becomes your genuine expression of worship. Stop imitating the ideals and opinions of the culture around you, but be inwardly transformed by the Holy Spirit through a total reformation of how you think. This will empower you to discern God's will as you live a beautiful life, satisfying and perfect in his eyes."

That is where I started.

I had to. I had nothing. I hated myself. I hated everything about me. I begged God to change my personality. I wasn't able to look in the mirror without gritting my teeth and looking away from my face. I cursed myself everytime I caught a glimpse.

I was too much…

When I was little I was always told that I talked too much. I was called "mouth of the south". I was called "little heffer". I was "over the top" all of my life, I was told. "You are such a spaz, Jenny." I was also known as a "blooming idiot". Not only did I carry those demeaning words on my identity, there was more to deal with… the body image damage.

As you probably know, when you grow up as someone who was abused as a child . . . your body is just not your friend.

For me, my body tagged along with me for obvious reasons, I lived in it and couldn't get away from it. I tolerated everything about it. I always picked myself apart. I always had a reason to not love me.

I will never forget when I looked into that mirror and, instead of being revolted by my own self-hatred, for the first time, I saw a little girl. It broke my heart. I was so abusive to who I saw in me. It helped me to see myself differently… to pull out little girl pictures of myself and place them where I could see them regularly. I just started talking to her and memorizing her. That was me!

I don't know how you feel about yourself. I don't know what things you say about yourself and what thoughts you come up against that keep you down. I just know that you probably treat you much worse than you treat anyone else. That can look like many different things. I do want to go into that more but not yet.

Instead, I want to link arms with you right now, partner with your Creator and speak into that.

Activations

Activation 1:

Let's go to Romans 12:1-2 (see above). In the morning, when you rise, go to the mirror and stay. Take captive your thoughts right away to make them obedient to your Captain, to your Lord Jesus.

It may look something like this:

Father, thank You for Your mercies this morning. (tell Him how you feel, it's ok!) I surrender myself to be a sacred, living sacrifice. Help me to live in holiness and experience all that delights Your heart. I want to genuinely worship you from that place of surrender, to please you.

I reject all cultural ideals and opinions around me but instead, will become inwardly transformed by the Holy Spirit and accept total transformation in how I think about You, myself and the world around me. I will also accept total transformation for how I think about all that has happened to me.

Holy Spirit, empower me to discern God's will as I live a beautiful life, satisfying and perfect in Your eyes. - Amen

Don't worry about not feeling anything when you go through that prayer. It takes time. Be nice to you. Give yourself time. But start there. Do it everyday until one day, you just do it naturally. The Holy Spirit will honor this in your life. I promise.

Also, there's something that I did for years and still catch myself doing but not as much. I hear women use degrading, negative, even hurtful language towards themselves that just breaks my heart.

Have you ever done that?

You probably do and don't even realize that you are doing it. Listen, when we open our mouths, we're either blessing or we are cursing.

It can sound like:

I hate my freckles. I hate my hair. Why are my eyes like that? My voice sounds weird. I am so fat. Ug, I wish I had boobs. My butt is too small. I could never do that. No one will ever love me. I am so stupid."

Sound familiar?

Listen for it. Try to catch it. Everytime you feel a certain way, stop talking. Turn your heart and mind and stop talking. Don't let that come out of your mouth.

Say this instead:

"Thank you God for giving me beautiful eyes to see all that you have made. Just reverse the curse that you almost put on yourself. Practice until one day, you just accept you and love you. Be held accountable to a friend. Ask them to call you out on what you are saying about yourself. Speak blessings over you! You are so valuable and such a treasure. There is no one in the world like you!

Activation 2:

Journal.

Find a friend to walk with you. Don't try to do this alone. It's a horrible way to live. Trust me, I know.

Let Him.

Just say yes. Say yes to Jesus. He is kind and gentle and oh, so loving.

Even when you want to die, say yes to Him. Even when your heart feels irreparable. You feel like you will never get to the other side. You will. I promise, if you will just let Jesus.

I am simply amazed at where God has brought me. My life is nothing short of a miracle and I am so happy. I am free and I love me. I love me in the sense of Psalm 139. I am fearfully and wonderfully made.

I belong to Jesus and that's pretty special. If He died for me, gave up everything for me, then who am I to turn on me? Does that make sense? If God's only Son thinks that highly of me, I'm pretty special.

My spiritual momma, Diane, sang a song to me that I want to sing over you right now. I needed it more than anything and when she looked me in the face and sang these words . . . it was just like healing balm over my broken and wounded soul.

"You are loved, you are beautiful, you're a gift from God - His own creation. You're a gift for all mankind, His gift of love to them. You are loved - God danced the day you were born."

I wish that I could take your hands and hold them in mine. I would love to wash you with the powerful truth of that special little song.

You are loved.

I just turned 48 and I am finally learning how to do self-care in a different arena.

I needed to do soul care first and then as my mind has been renewed more and more, I'm able to do another kind of self-care. I am allowing myself the freedom to stumble and make mistakes. I am learning how to be easy on me… To give myself grace. To walk away from stress and triggers.

It's ok. I have permission to step away from toxic people and toxic situations but I do not have permission to mistreat me or anyone else. Walk away. Take a minute or a week!

I love my new daily beauty regimens and weight loss success. I'm on a journey to become healthier.

Why?

Because I decided to do it for myself. I am learning how to use oils and creams and all kinds of beautiful feminine products. It's me on the other side of the hell that I never thought I'd escape!

Jesus - thank you for the precious heart that is reading this right this minute. Thank you for dying for her so that she can walk in the abundance of life that you want her to walk in. Free her. Show her what you see in her. Break every chain.

Do it Jesus.

Amen

So now…

…go and get that pedicure. Wash your hair in that sudsy, fragrant shampoo and do your hair today. Take a walk. Call a friend. Send yourself a card to tell that little inner girl that she is special and how sorry you are for treating her so badly. Enjoy a cup of coffee. Relax and let Him.

I love you.

Chapter 25

Authenticity

If you don't want to be misunderstood, then avoid living authentically.

If you live with an open heart and authentically you will be misunderstood. If you are not hiding, you will be misunderstood. Most people are hiding and when you meet someone who is not hiding it can often be unsettling to those who are hiding.

Crying and breaking before the Lord is not a weakness, it's actually a strength gained through humility and an acknowledgement that we can't even breathe without Him lending us that breath!

Authentic living is not about other people. I have learned, along the way, that it's not about glass house living, it's how you live before the Lord… being real with yourself in and about every season. It's about being real with Jesus.

When I listen to little children, I hear true authenticity. When I see them, I see authenticity. I once thought that authenticity meant that I tell every little detail about everything that I have ever gone through.

But I learned the hard way… that is actually foolishness. So, I learned to keep my pearls very close.

When we live in the light with the Father, knowing that He sees, hears, knows and cares so deeply, that's where healing really begins.

Keep your pearls close, darling. Let Jesus walk with you. You can trust Him and you can live in an authentic way with Him.

Activation

This is a great place to begin practicing two things toward others: self-control and journaling. If you haven't started journaling yet, now is the time. Put it all out there—every messy detail, and all the good stuff too. Write, cry, yell, scream, weep—just get it out. And keep it close. These are your pearls. When you feel the urge to be understood… shhhh. Keep it close.

There will come a time when the Lord will help you release your testimony, but not too soon.

Years ago I was manipulated by a pastor of a church to come and tell my story in front of his congregation. I said no so many times but he called and called and called. He said to me that he will not take no for an answer and so I reluctantly said yes.

I bombed. It was a set up. I stood in front of all of these people and a lady walked in dressed like she was going to a bar, showing all kinds of skin and cleavage. This was my biggest trigger. I was triggered and it was cruel. I began to weep and I froze and I said . . . I cannot do this. I ran.

This pastor was angry with me and I never heard from him again. I spiralled backwards. This is where I started to understand the importance of my precious pearls and it is why I can share this with you.

Lord, please give me wisdom. Help me with controlling the desire to be understood and known. I ask you for discretion and also the courage to say no when I need to. Help me to be able to set strong boundaries while you heal me. Fence me in. Hem me in, Jesus.

"for the light makes everything visible. This is why it is said,
"Awake, O sleeper,
  rise up from the dead,
  and Christ will give you light." (Ephesians 5:14 NLT)

Chapter 26

The Language Of Heaven

A House Full of Holes and a Heart Full of Complaints...

When I talk about getting away from a critical spirit, I mean all of it. The voice inside of you. The voices around you. Critical people. Critical thoughts. Negative environments. It's hard to move away from that kind of heaviness if you don't even realize it's there.

Years ago, my family moved to a small town in Ohio. We were still young parents. Our daughter was twelve, we had a toddler and we had a newborn baby. We moved into a house that was, well - falling apart. The fence looked like a row of broken teeth. Outbuildings were rotted, collapsing in places. One wall had a hole the size of a basketball that led from the outside straight into our kitchen - right under the stove.

We didn't own the house; we were renting it from someone we knew. They painted us a Mayberry picture, but the reality was far from that. I didn't work outside the home, and my husband did the best he could to provide for us.

We had made the decision to live simply, and it was a sacrifice, but it was our decision.

Still, I hated that house.

I complained about everything - out loud, constantly. The floors. The walls. The mold. The mice. The fact that nothing seemed clean or right. I had picked up a critical spirit, and I didn't even realize how deep it had gotten.

At some point, six or seven years in, I heard myself. Really heard myself. And it was ugly. Disgusting. I repented before God and then apologized to my husband.

That was the beginning of change.

My husband said something wise, "Since you don't love being inside the house, why don't we create something outside that brings you joy?"

And we did.

We made a beautiful outdoor room with twinkle lights, flowers, comfy furniture, and soft music. We spent hours out there - family time, quiet time, company time. That outdoor room became a sanctuary.

It was in that broken-down house where I learned to be thankful.

And not just outwardly. I had to recognize that the most critical person I knew… was me. That house didn't change right away. But my language did.

I started naming the good.

I thanked God for my family, for my salvation, for the things we did have. And not long after that, we got a call. The owners wanted their son to move in. Not because we did anything wrong - it was just time.

Looking back, I believe God let us stay there until I learned the holy weight of thanksgiving. I had to understand that complaining attracts darkness, but gratitude draws in the light. You enter His gates with thanksgiving (Psalm 100:4).

So if you're constantly complaining and criticizing - whose gates are you entering?

This was a major part of my healing: learning to change my language. I still have to fight for it, especially when I don't feel well. I'm a verbal processor, so when I'm not careful, everything spills out of my mouth.

Now, I remind myself, "If you can't speak with thanksgiving, be silent until you can."

Activation

Shift the Atmosphere

Start by paying attention to your words. What do people hear when you speak? Do your words carry hope or heaviness?

Then, speak three things out loud that you're thankful for. If you can't think of three, say one. One is enough to start.

Examples:

"God, thank You for my salvation."

"Thank You for Jesus."

"Thank You for my family."

"Thank You for the breath in my lungs."

"Thank You for the tree outside my window."

There is always something to be thankful for. Shift the atmosphere of your heart by "speaking life."

Prayer

Lord, I thank You for my friend holding this book. Thank You for their desire to grow, to heal, and to walk in freedom. Help them to hear their own words and recognize any language that's tearing down instead of building up.

Remind them of the beauty in their life, even if it's just one small thing today.

Teach us to enter Your gates with thanksgiving, and to speak heaven's language over ourselves and our homes.

Thank You, Jesus, for Your mercy.

Thank You for Your blood.

Thank You for never giving up on us.

Amen.

Chapter 27

Find Your People

What does it mean to glean from someone?

1. To take that which has been left behind, usually grain remaining after a harvest. A noun or pronoun can be used between "glean" and "from." How much grain were you able to glean from the fields today?

2. To learn something from a particular source, often secondhand or piecemeal. https://idioms.thefreedictionary.com/glean+from+(something)

I was lonely. I was hungry and I was scared. I used to dream of relationships. I had such a deep longing to fellowship deeply. I didn't know how to go about it. I was overwhelmed and therefore I was overwhelming to others.

When I got back into church after years of not being in church, I was excited to have that connection. I learned the church language and I learned how to "talk the talk". I had read a lot of scripture in my life and it was in there. I liked to use scripture in every situation . . . only not for the right reasons. I was hiding, and if I thought for a second that you "saw" me, I ran.

I was talking to Jesus one day about friends. I asked Him why I didn't have any.

You know what He said to me?

"If you want a friend, learn how to be one first."

That stuck with me! I watched Jesus and how He was a friend to me. It has taken me many years, but I can honestly tell you that now, I am a wonderful friend.

I have thought about this frequently in the past and I still think about this often. I will tell you that you have to be really careful when you are loving and serving people. If you find yourself giving to people or serving people and loving people and they are not reciprocating this back to you, be careful that you're not getting offended. But it will happen! You will get offended. You will get hurt.

It's ok when you get hurt because it will teach you about who your people are. This is where finding your people really begins.

I was never good at shallow conversation and so I would freak people out by going right for the jugular. I wanted deep because deep calls to the deep. I had been so deeply hurt and as I began to heal and feel things, I wanted others to participate in my journey.

Being hurt and rejected along the way, I learned who my people were. The deep water people stuck with me through the years. I like to call them covenant relationships. I have friends and acquaintances and then I have "my people".

This is crucial for deeper healing.

You also will learn along the way that your people will look for the gems inside of you and call them out. Your people will pray for you and will learn your language and you will learn theirs.

To bring more practical clarity on this, let me give you an example of what happened to me years ago and what a covenant relationship looks like.

My husband and I had moved farther away from the friends that I had. Maybe 2 hours away. I was deeply and intensely lonely during this move. I was walking out of the grocery store one blustery winter evening. It was dark and so cold. As I walked to my car I related to that blustery, dark, cold night. It was lonely, more than I have ever felt.

Over the next few days I remembered what the Lord had told me about how to have a friend. I looked up a local church and made my way over there.

There were life group fliers on the wall and I grabbed the one that was labeled "Women's Bible Study". I called Sharon the next day. It took a few days for her to get back to me and when she did call, it was short and sweet.

She invited me to her home. I found out that she had asked the leaders to take her flier down previously. It was officially a full and closed group. But for God's divine plan in my life, it was not taken down and I was connected to one of the most valuable relationships I have ever known. It was no accident!

That was a long time ago and we are still sitting at the Table together. She became one of the most significant people who the Lord has used to heal me. I am still meeting new people and making new friends all because of that flier that should have been taken down. My husband says . . . "it was going to happen".

Later on, I was sitting in a ladies prayer group with Sharon and a lot of women who were much older than me. My husband needed my car for something and so he dropped me off. Mid meeting, I was triggered by something and I went into panic mode. Also, the enemy was feeding me lies! I said to these ladies . . . do you really like me? Are you going to reject me? Sharon looked at me (in the particular way that only Sharon can) and said, "Jennifer, what are you talking about?"

I stayed. They stayed and I learned how to trust and grow. I have learned how to listen and be vulnerable. I have learned who my people are. I have also allowed the Table to grow because now there are women coming who are just like where I was 20 years ago. And I get to love them!

These are my people and you will find yours.

Activation

One step at a time, one day at a time, laugh your laugh. Cry your cry. Be yourself. You are beautiful. It's hard when you are hurt but it is a tool in your tool belt. Let Jesus show you who your people are. Ask Him to highlight them. I know it is so basic, but so often we forget to invite Him into these intimate things.

"Such wicked people are detestable to the LORD, but he offers his friendship to the godly." (Proverbs 3:32 NLT)

"I tell you, use worldly wealth to gain friends for yourselves, so that when it is gone, you will be welcomed into eternal dwellings." (Luke 16:9 NIV)

"Perfume and incense bring joy to the heart, and the pleasantness of a friend springs from their heartfelt advice." (Proverbs 27:9 NIV)

The Lord loves me. The Lord wants to trust me with His friendship. Take your time darling. Let Jesus show you how to be a friend and also what to look for in a friend.

Jesus, my friend. Even when I am not… you are. Show me what it is like to be a friend and highlight to me who my people are so that I can heal.

Precious one. I am your friend and I want to encourage you to not settle for less than what God has for you. You are His prize and He will show you all that you need to know.

Chapter 28

Trust

And finally friends - trust.

We need to talk about this.

Trust isn't something that we give away. It's something that we gradually GIFT to someone who has earned it.

Trust is a gift. Trust is earned.

It took me many, many years to learn this.

All my life, I wanted to be understood and known - but I went about it the wrong way. I thought the only way to be understood and known was to tell everyone my deepest, my most personal gems…

I shared ME with people who often did not deserve that.

I didn't understand the value of my gems at that stage in my healing journey.

And because I didn't appreciate the value of me, or my gems, I didn't have the discretion to protect myself from people who did not yet prove they deserved access.

I finally learned the detriment of that a few years ago when I was completely sabotaged and betrayed by someone I thought was my friend.

I was invited to an event that she was having, and I was nervous about going because of who might be there. I was tossed back and forth between going and not going.

I cared about her and decided to share with her why I may or may not attend. I knew it would depend on the strength of my heart that day and my mental state.

I decided to be completely honest with her.

This was a bad move.

I trusted her - but she didn't have the compassion or the empathy that was necessary for what I shared with her.

I was so hurt that she seemed to neither care nor understand what I had shared.

It crushed me, and our relationship was in trouble. I loved her and wanted to be sure that we were "OK."

A few months later, rumors started swirling around, and it got back to me that she had shared my treasure with others.

She broke confidence - and it felt like a hot blade in my back, twisting and twisting, until I finally woke up one day (a few years later) and decided:

I don't want to be a part of any gossiping community.

It's time to forgive, heal, and move on.

I am now able to encourage my children and friends in this area of trust.

Trust...

The definition of trust taken from the Oxford English Dictionary and Merriam-Webster is:

"firm belief in the reliability, truth, ability, or strength of someone or something."

Read that again and feel the weight of it.

It is a big deal to be able to trust someone - and also to be trusted.

Are you trustworthy?

For those of us who have been betrayed in the most heinous way possible, it is a miracle that we would ever learn to trust in a pure way.

Trust is not the same as just putting your "junk" in front of people just to be understood.

This is immature and ignorant.

I can say that because I learned the hard way.

Scripture tells us to put our complete trust in the Lord:

"Trust in the Lord with all your heart and lean not on your own understanding; in all your ways submit to him, and he will make your paths straight." (Proverbs 3:5-6 NIV)

Sadly, so many of us don't learn healthy trust growing up.

We don't understand the true meaning or the responsibility.

When you grow up in an environment where abuse is present - whether it's physical, emotional, sexual, or even spiritual - you learn to survive, not trust.

You learn to read the room, please everyone, become the scapegoat, or stay invisible.

You learn how to protect yourself, how to keep secrets, how to smile when you're numb. But you don't learn how to trust.

Because trust was never safe.

You may have been taught that trust is earned - but the people who were supposed to earn it never did. And yet, you were still expected to hand it over.

So, you grow up confused.

You either don't trust anyone, or you trust too quickly and too deeply because you're just so desperate for someone to trust. You overshare, or you never share. You carry the weight of secrets that weren't yours to hold.

And then one day, you find yourself asking, "Why does trust feel so hard for me?"

If that's you, I want you to know this: you're not broken.

You were taught to survive in an environment that failed to protect you. And now - slowly - you are longing for something more holy, something more whole.

You're learning what trust really is.

You're learning that it starts with God.

And from there, you learn how to GIFT it - with discernment, with wisdom, and with peace.

Activation

Take a few moments and ask yourself:

Who has earned my trust - and why?

Have I been giving away parts of myself to people who have not proven trustworthy?

Am I creating a safe place for others to trust me?

What does trusting God really look like in my daily life?

Now write a letter to your younger self - the version of you who didn't understand trust yet.

Be kind. Be honest. Tell her what she needs to know now about trust, betrayal, and healing.

Let this be part of your restoration.

Prayer

Jesus,

You are the One who never betrays, never breaks confidence, and never wounds with intention.

Teach me how to trust again - starting with You.

Heal the places in me that still ache from betrayal.

Help me become a person who is trustworthy, steady, and wise.

I forgive those who didn't know how to hold my story well.

And I ask You to hold the pieces of me that feel scattered.

Make my heart whole again.

Amen.

Chapter 29

Trembling Into Trust

I have lived through a lot of abuse and trauma and I was rough. God's love has softened me over time. He has helped me begin to trust. But I'm still slow and discreet with people - and honestly, that's probably wise.

I'm growing.

Hypervigilance is the experience of living in a high state of alert - a constant tension, a never-ending watchfulness. You're always scanning for danger, whether real or imagined. It's exhausting to live that way, and it's exhausting for the people closest to you.

And here's the truth - hypervigilance often walks hand-in-hand with PTSD.

Let's talk about that for a minute.

Post-traumatic stress disorder isn't just something military veterans deal with. It happens to victims of trauma - period. And when it happens, it's devastating.

PTSD shows up in the life of someone who is struggling to recover after witnessing or experiencing something terrifying. The condition can last for months or even years, and certain triggers can bring those memories right back, along with intense emotional and physical reactions.

My PTSD lasted many years.

Symptoms can include nightmares, intrusive thoughts, anxiety, avoidance of certain places or people, irrational fears, hypersensitivity, and deep sadness. It looks different for each of us, but it always takes a toll.

Let me be clear - I won't recommend medical treatments in this book. That's a personal decision, and only you can make that choice. I'll just tell you what I did - and for me, I chose not to take psychotropic medication. I do believe that godly counseling is beneficial. But choose wisely.

Hypervigilance and PTSD showed up in every part of my healing journey - especially in my marriage. It felt like nearly everything triggered me. The fact that Aaron is a man made me feel unsafe. He couldn't approach me from behind, raise his hands around me, or even look in the direction of another woman without me melting down. I was constantly afraid. Constantly triggered.

But eventually, I came to this:

I wanted to trust him.

And I knew, deep down, I was safe with him.

So I made the decision to agree with God - that my husband is a good man. I said it out loud until I believed it. And while I'm still learning to trust, I want to trust - because Aaron is trustworthy. He has never given me a reason not to trust him. And I'm thankful for him.

My triggers reminded me of moments when I was helpless - when I had no voice, no power, no escape. But healing came when I began acknowledging that I'm not that helpless girl anymore. I'm not in danger. I can speak up. I can say no. I can leave if I need to.

Before I learned that I had a choice, I reacted in ways that terrified my husband. I've said things. Done things. Hurt him. I've been irrational. I have painful memories of treating him badly because I was afraid.

Honestly, marriage is where PTSD can hurt the most.

When I was single, it was easier to manage these kinds of things. I could work, drink, shop, or exercise until I numbed the pain and felt something remotely good. I kept people at a distance. No people meant no pain. And that worked - until I met Aaron.

He knew something awful had happened to me, but he didn't know the details. Early in our marriage, he realized I was a mess. Honestly, it's a miracle we're still together after two decades.

But we are.

Because he showed me love - pure, godly love.

And that kind of love helped save me.

If you're walking through this - if you're experiencing PTSD and constant triggering - please consider seeking godly counseling. I'm very specific in saying godly counseling. I had a few counselors along the way, and I was extremely careful about who I let in. This is a sacred journey, and you don't owe anyone access to your healing.

This is the time to be picky. Be wise. Be guarded. Protect your pearls.

Activation

When you're triggered, pause. Practice speaking to your heart and emotions. Step away and talk yourself down. Cry. Scream. Hit a pillow if you need to. Just breathe.

Deep breathing can calm your body and emotions. If you're in a truly safe space, take a look around. Name what's beautiful. Smell something fragrant. Touch something soft - your shirt, your blanket, your pet. These grounding tools help anchor you in the present.

If you're not in a safe place, move immediately. You don't need permission.

And please - journal. Journal what you feel. Journal what you want. Journal what you can't say out loud yet.

When I was in intense emotional pain, my husband wrote a song I sang over and over:

"Heal me, and I will be healed. Save me, and I will be saved. For You are my King."

Some days, I couldn't pray anything but that—and sometimes just one word:

Help.

Find a Psalm to cling to. My go-to was Psalm 139. It reminded me that my life matters. That God sees me, knows me, and understands the pain I don't have words for.

And here are some scriptures to meditate on:

Psalm 139 – You Know All About Me

"I pray with great faith for you, because I'm fully convinced that the One who began this gracious work in you will faithfully continue the process of maturing you until the unveiling of our Lord Jesus Christ!" (Philippians 1:6 TPT)

"And it's true: "Everyone who calls on the Lord's name will experience new life." (Romans 10:13 TPT)

You are deeply loved.
I'm so sorry you're walking through this kind of pain.
But if you will stay with the process - you will be healed.
You will be saved.
God will finish what He started in you.

Prayer

Jesus, this isn't something we were ever meant to walk through - and yet, here we are.

The choices of others have caused us deep pain. Our very identity has been assaulted. And we cannot walk through this alone.

I lift up the one holding this book, reading this page, crying these tears.
Catch her heart, Jesus. What a treasure the human heart is - it's Your prize.

As she walks through triggers, PTSD, and hypervigilance, I ask for clarity, wisdom, and a friend who will be like Jesus in human form for them. It's so easy to feel alone and sad while still being expected to perform and produce in this world.

We need You. Every moment of every day.

Thank You for Your constant love and constant counsel.

Amen.

SECTION FOUR: Redemption & Restoration

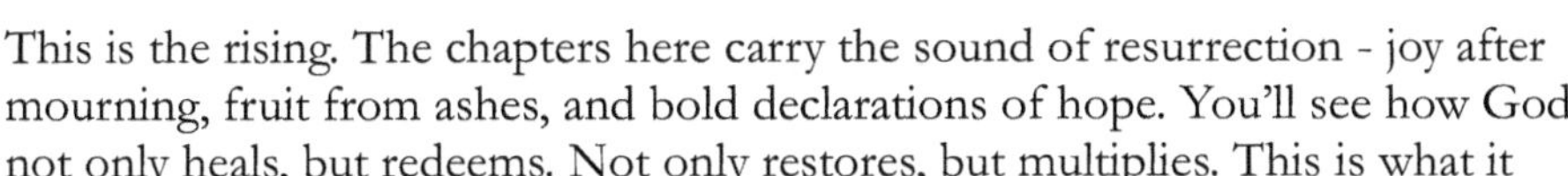

This is the rising. The chapters here carry the sound of resurrection - joy after mourning, fruit from ashes, and bold declarations of hope. You'll see how God not only heals, but redeems. Not only restores, but multiplies. This is what it looks like when love has the final word.

Chapter 30

Joy Comes In The Mourning

Joy.

Joy is not about happiness.

Happiness is great, but in this life, we are not promised happiness. Are we?

Joy and happiness…

Let's see what the Word says about joy.

"Take delight in the Lord, and he will give you the desires of your heart." **Joy comes when we delight in the Lord!** (Psalms 37:4 NIV)

"Consider it pure joy, my brothers and sisters, whenever you face trials of many kinds, because you know that the testing of your faith produces perseverance." **Joy comes with perseverance!** (James 1:2-3 NIV)

"Go ahead and celebrate! Come on and clap your hands, everyone! Shout to God with the raucous sounds of joy!" **Joy comes with praise and worship!** (Psalms 47:1 TPT)

"You have enlarged the nation and increased their joy; they rejoice before you as people rejoice at the harvest, as warriors rejoice when dividing the plunder." **Joy comes with victory!** (Isaiah 9:3 NIV)

"Go, eat your food with gladness, and drink your wine with a joyful heart, for God has already approved what you do." **Joy comes with freedom!** (Ecclesiastes 9:7 NIV)

"Lovers of God have a joyful feast of gladness, but the ungodly see their hopes vanish right before their eyes." **Joy comes with being glad!** (Proverbs 10:28 TPT)

"You love him passionately although you have not seen him, but through believing in him you are saturated with an ecstatic joy, indescribably sublime and immersed in glory. For you are reaping the harvest of your faith—the full salvation promised you—your souls' victory!" **Joy comes from believing God!** (1 Peter 1:8-9 TPT)

"Now may God, the fountain of hope, fill you to overflowing with uncontainable joy and perfect peace as you trust in him. And may the power of the Holy Spirit continually surround your life with his super-abundance until you radiate with hope!" **Joy comes with being filled with the Holy Spirit!** (Romans 15:13 TPT)

"Although I have many more subjects I'd like to discuss with you, I'd rather not include them in this letter. But I look forward to coming to visit and speaking with you face-to-face —for being together will complete our joy!" **Joy comes with unity!** (2 John 1:12 TPT)

"Jesus continued, "In the same way, there will be a glorious celebration in heaven over the rescue of one lost sinner who repents, comes back home, and returns to the fold—more so than for all the righteous people who never strayed away."" **Joy comes when we celebrate others!** (Luke 15:7 TPT)

"Nehemiah said, "Go and enjoy choice food and sweet drinks, and send some to those who have nothing prepared. This day is holy to our Lord. Do not grieve, for the joy of the Lord is your strength."" **The joy of the Lord is your strength!** (Nehemiah 8:10 NIV)

"In every province and in every city to which the edict of the king came, there was joy and gladness among the Jews, with feasting and celebrating. And many people of other nationalities became Jews because fear of the Jews had seized them." **Joy comes in the presence of our King!** (Esther 8:17 NIV)

"Shout aloud and sing for joy, people of Zion, for great is the Holy One of Israel among you."" **Joy comes in our praise and our song for Jesus!** (Isaiah 12:6 NIV)

"Your love has given me great joy and encouragement, because you, brother, have refreshed the hearts of the Lord's people." **Joy comes when we know and believe He loves us**!
Philemon 1:7 NIV

"In the day of trouble, he will treasure me in his shelter, under the cover of his tent. He will lift me high upon a rock, out of reach from all my enemies who surround me. Triumphant now, I'll bring him my offerings of praise, singing and shouting with ecstatic joy! Yes, I will sing praises to Yahweh!" **Joy comes when we praise Him!** (Psalms 27:5-6 TPT)

"and those the Lord has rescued will return. They will enter Zion with singing; everlasting joy will crown their heads. Gladness and joy will overtake them, and sorrow and sighing will flee away." **Joy comes when we're rescued!** (Isaiah 35:10 NIV)

"Everyone enjoys giving great advice. But how delightful it is to say the right thing at the right time!" **Joy comes when we encourage others in the spirit!** (Proverbs 15:23 TPT)

"So with you: Now is your time of grief, but I will see you again and you will rejoice, and no one will take away your joy." **Joy is always ours!** (John 16:22 NIV)

"I've learned that his anger lasts for a moment, but his loving favor lasts a lifetime! We may weep through the night, but at daybreak it will turn into shouts of ecstatic joy." **Joy comes in the morning!** (Psalms 30:5 TPT)

"For the kingdom of God is not a matter of rules about food and drink, but is in the realm of the Holy Spirit, filled with righteousness, peace, and joy." **Joy belongs to the Kingdom of God! (**Romans 14:17 TPT)

"We look away from the natural realm and we focus our attention and expectation onto Jesus who birthed faith within us and who leads us forward into faith's perfection. His example is this: Because his heart was focused on the joy of knowing that you would be his, he endured the agony of the cross and conquered its humiliation, and now sits exalted at the right hand of the throne of God!" **Read this out loud. Jesus had Joy in his suffering because He had His heart focused on you and that you would be His. (**Hebrews 12:2 TPT)

What does joy in the ***mourning*** really mean?

Joy is not the denial of grief.

It's not pretending everything's fine. It doesn't mean you don't have pain.

Joy is anchored.

It doesn't shift with our emotions. It's rooted in God's presence, not our circumstances.

You can have tears on your face and still have joy in your soul.

You can be in a season of loss, and still have a hope that holds.

You can be misunderstood, betrayed, broken—and somehow, mysteriously, miraculously—still held by joy. And it really is a miracle!

Not because life is easy. But because God is near and He loves you.

The Word is clear: joy isn't optional for the believer—it's promised. It shows up in the wilderness, in the prison cell, in the grief, in the healing, in the waiting. Joy doesn't cancel mourning. It coexists with it. And eventually—if we stay near to Him—joy outlasts it.

Activation

Take 10–15 minutes this week and sit with the Scriptures above. Let them speak to you.

Then ask yourself:

Have I believed that joy and mourning couldn't live in the same space?

What do I really believe joy is?

What grief am I carrying that needs to be met with God's joy?

What would it look like to "eat with joy" again? To drink with joy again? To walk and dance with joy again? To sing, to praise, to believe again?

Write a declaration over yourself:

"I will have joy, even here. Even now."

What places are you hurting? What places are you grieving? Ask Jesus to meet you in these places with His joy.

His joy is your strength.

Then say it out loud.

Prayer

Lord,
You are the God who gives beauty for ashes and joy for mourning.
You are near to the brokenhearted, and You promise that weeping may last for the night, but joy comes in the morning.

Even when my heart is heavy, I know joy is possible—not because of what I feel, but because of who You are.

So God, would You meet me in my mourning?

Would You remind me of the joy that cannot be taken, the joy that rises from Your presence?

I say yes to it, even if it feels far. I say yes to joy as an act of trust.

Thank You for holding both my sorrow and my joy.

Amen

Chapter 31

All Things New

I don't know about you, but I'm tired. Yes, I'm mentally drained from a long day of working with needy people. Yes, I'm tired and didn't exactly "feel" like running right home to serve my family. But - not just that kinda tired. I'm tired.

I'm tired of the inner struggle. I'm tired of that inner struggle! Do you know what I'm talking about? I'm tired of the push and pull and the tug of war between my spirit and my flesh. I'm sick of it!

I ate too much… or, I had one glass too many, or I lost my temper, or I don't want to "snuggle" with my husband and I don't want my kids to ask me one more thing right now.

I don't want to listen to anyone!

I'm tired of how I feel in my skin and well, I'm just tired. Does any of this resonate with you? Oh, and how about the seemingly endless arguments that cycle through your mind when someone has hurt you or offended you. You know, that argument that you have with them in your head because they are wrong . . . and you're not.

My personal favorite is guilt. Guilt, for not being a perfect mom; wish I had treated my mother better, wish I had hugged my husband before bed last night, wish I hadn't snapped at my friend . . . that kind of guilt. Not good enough. "I suck" because my children struggle. That's my favorite.

"So I find this law at work: Although I want to do good, evil is right there with me. For in my inner being I delight in God's law; but I see another law at work in me, waging war against the law of my mind and making me a prisoner of the law of sin at work within me. What a wretched man I am! Who will rescue me from this body that is subject to death? Thanks be to God, who delivers me through Jesus Christ our Lord!" (Romans 7: 21-25 TPT)

That's how I'm feeling tonight. Guilty! Heavy. Waiting. Waiting for everything to settle down inside of me so that I can feel somewhat normal again. Or is this normal? I believe that for now, on earth, in this body, yes. Until I am internally restored, this is the battle of being human and living inside of dirt. Ecclesiastes 3:20

I came across this tonight and it was just in time.

No more sorrow. No more suffering. No more death. No more cause for mourning. When all things are made new, our hearts will finally be free from grief. The joy of that moment will eclipse even the physical healing we long for. Just imagine—if God offered today to take away your deepest inner wounds, what would you ask Him to lift from you?

And once it was gone—once that wound was healed—what would your joy be like?

No more tears. No more pain. No more death. No more mourning. When the renewal of all things comes—just as God has promised—our hearts will be finally and fully free from grief. "He will wipe every tear from their eyes. There will be no more death or mourning or crying or pain" (Revelation 21:4 NIV).

And the joy of that moment—the joy of restoration—will far outweigh even the relief we once longed for in our bodies. "I consider that our present sufferings are not worth comparing with the glory that will be revealed in us" (Romans 8:18 NIV).

Activation

Today is a new day! Say this every time you begin to feel lingering emotions. For example, when guilt or shame starts to creep in, say: Today is a new day. And then, choose to believe God when He says His mercies are new everyday.

"Forget the former things; do not dwell on the things of the past." (Isaiah 43:18 NIV)

"See, I am doing a new thing!
Now it springs up; do you not perceive it?
I am making a way in the wilderness
and streams in the wasteland." (Isaiah 43:19 NIV)

He who was seated on the throne said, "I am making everything new!" Then he said, "Write this down, for these words are trustworthy and true." (Revelation 21:5 NIV)

"See, I will create
new heavens and a new earth.
The former things will not be remembered,
nor will they come to mind.... (Isaiah 65:17 NIV)

God promises over and over that He IS making ALL things new. I WILL make ALL things new. I AM doing a new thing.

We have to begin to believe Him and take God at His word. His Word is faithful and True.

If you will press on and allow yourself to begin to believe that He is good and He is for you . . .
Eventually you will see hope springing up like a bubbling brook.

Lord, I need you. I need hope. I need to believe that you are doing a new thing, and will do a new thing. I need you to pull me up and catch my heart when I begin to lose hope.

Jesus, thank you for loving me. Help me believe.

Chapter 32

Fruit

No matter what we've been through in life, there's a promise of fruit that we can never produce on our own.

"But the fruit produced by the Holy Spirit within you is divine love in all its varied expressions: joy that overflows, peace that subdues, patience that endures, kindness in action, a life full of virtue, faith that prevails, gentleness of heart, and strength of spirit. Never set the law above these qualities, for they are meant to be limitless." (Galatians 5:22–23 TPT)

As we yield to the Holy Spirit more and more, we begin to experience more and more of His fruit.

In my life, I've learned that I need specific fruit in certain seasons more than others. The fruit of the Holy Spirit is always in season, but it becomes obvious: when I'm struggling with patience, I need patience. When there seems to be no joy in my life, it's apparent that I need joy. When I'm having a hard time getting out of myself or dealing with others, I need kindness.

We have to understand—we cannot produce this fruit on our own. This is not the fruit of Jennifer. This is the fruit of the Holy Spirit, and I depend on Him to produce it in me.

"The behavior of the self-life is obvious: sexual immorality, lustful thoughts, pornography, chasing after things instead of God, manipulating others, hatred of those who get in your way, senseless arguments, resentment when others are favored, temper tantrums, angry quarrels, only thinking of yourself, being in love with your own opinions, being envious of the blessings of others, murder, uncontrolled addictions, wild parties, and all other similar behavior. Haven't I already warned you that those who use their 'freedom' for these things will not inherit the kingdom realm of God!" (Galatians 5:19–21 TPT)

So how do we yield fruit if the fruit doesn't belong to us?

We yield. We surrender. We submit. We trust. We ask. We believe.

As I grow closer to the Lord, I begin to recognize this delicious fruit more and more in my life. It's also becoming more noticeable to others who come around me. On my own, I clearly struggle with impatience. When I'm tempted to lose my mind on someone, that's when I know I need to keep my mouth shut and pull back. That's when I need to close my eyes, allow my heart to realign, and ask the Holy Spirit to help me.

Years ago, my husband and I attended a small group at a church where we were active. There was a woman in the group who really tested my self-control and patience. She talked constantly. From the moment she arrived, she dominated the entire time. This was very difficult for me.

Even though I wasn't rude and never said anything, I could feel the impatience under my skin. I don't know if that makes sense, but for me, impatience feels like agitation just beneath the surface, ready to come out of my mouth. What I wanted to say was, "Can you please stop talking!?"

That was when I really began learning about the fruit of the Spirit.

I had to close my eyes and yield myself to the Holy Spirit. It was hard... sometimes I had to step outside to breathe.

On top of that, she was toxic. And when I say toxic, I mean she constantly complained, she was critical, and much of what came out of her mouth was vile. It was sad to me that the group leaders didn't step in. She controlled the atmosphere whenever she showed up.

At the time, I didn't understand that I could lean back into all this delicious fruit. I didn't realize I had full access to love, patience, gentleness, and kindness.

That season of my life taught me that this low-hanging fruit is always available to me—anytime, anywhere. But it took years of practice. I haven't perfected surrendering, but I've become more consistent in trusting the Holy Spirit to bear fruit in me.

In the Kingdom, so much is upside-down or counter-intuitive to our natural thinking. I have learned that low-hanging fruit is easy, light and always accessible but it's only through humility (going low) and surrender that we can experience it.

The world we live in is so demanding... the constant chatter, the noise in the atmosphere, the stuff going on inside our own souls. Something is always pulling at our attention. Something is always trying to draw us away.

Activation

I'm including an activation that I hope will help you face the struggles you're dealing with now—and those that may come in the future.

Be encouraged: if you're struggling with impatience, you have access to patience. If self-control feels out of reach, it's already available to you.

Here is a simple PRAYER Acronym framework to help you remember and apply this process any time you feel the overwhelm coming on.

1. **P - Pause**:

   The next time you feel overwhelmed, frustrated, or empty—pause. Take one deep breath.

2. **R - Recognize** (Acknowledge):

   Name the struggle: "I'm impatient right now." "I feel out of control." "I don't have peace."

3. **A - Ask**:

   Whisper this simple prayer:

   "Holy Spirit, I can't produce this on my own. But You can. I receive Your [patience, peace, love—whatever is needed]."

4. **Y - Yield**:

   Imagine yourself handing over the struggle to Him. Physically open your hands if it helps. Let Him lead.

5. **E - Engage** (Respond):

   What does surrender look like in this moment? It could be silence instead of a sharp word. Stillness instead of striving. Gentleness instead of reacting. Choose His way.

6. **R - Reflect**:

   At the end of your day, take a moment to journal:

When did I sense the Holy Spirit today? What fruit did I see growing in me? Where do I still need to yield?

Whatever it is you're lacking, the Holy Spirit has everything you need. The key is learning to surrender - moment by moment, choice by choice.

Holy Spirit,

I pray for the one reading this right now. You see every struggle, every moment of weakness, every place they feel like they're not enough. Thank You that You are more than enough.

I ask that You would meet them right where they are—in the middle of the mess, the questions, the weariness, or even the numbness. Remind them that they don't have to produce this fruit on their own. It's not their strength. It's Yours.

When they're impatient, be their patience. When they feel like they're failing, remind them of Your faithfulness. Grow gentleness in them, joy in them, peace in them. Let love overflow and self-control be their anchor.

Teach them how to yield in the everyday moments. Whisper truth when they want to give up. Lead them into deeper trust and daily surrender.

May Your fruit be so alive in them that it begins to change the atmosphere around them. Not for show—but for Your glory. In Jesus' name, amen.

Don't leave the Holy Spirit out of your life.

"And don't get drunk with wine, which is rebellion; instead be filled continually with the Holy Spirit." (Ephesians 5:18 TPT)

"Remember, it is the same Holy Spirit who distributes, activates, and operates these different gifts as he chooses for each believer." (1 Corinthians 12:11 TPT)

Chapter 33

Hope

The first thing that I want to instill into you is hope. Without it, you will not make it. Hope gives us something to look forward to. It gives us vision and possibilities for a future.

Have you ever found yourself drawn to something morbid or negative and you can't seem to pull yourself away from it? There isn't any hope in that, friend. That will suck the life out of you.

Keep your thoughts continually fixed on all that is authentic and real, honorable and admirable, beautiful and respectful, pure and holy, merciful and kind. And fasten your thoughts on every glorious work of God, praising him always. (Philippians 4:8 TPT)

Recently I came across someone on social media that I can't say I know. I know what she has done and I met her once. I immediately didn't like her, all of those years ago. I was scrolling and caught myself in a critical place. I told myself to get out of that and I didn't.

I wanted to see what she might be about these days. She caused a lot of unnecessary pain in my life. I heard the Holy Spirit say to me, " you two would be good friends". I smiled and agreed.

Suddenly, my heart switched towards her. I decided that I no longer needed to feel anything negative and that I am forever free from that. I am not the same person that I was back then. And the Holy Spirit is right . . . we'd be good friends.

It's so important for us to be careful about what we are sinking our emotions into… what we read, listen to, who we receive advice from, what we allow ourselves to be a part of on social media, etc. We need to be very intentional about what we allow in through our "gates".

It's too expensive to be passive!

There was a time when I had no control over my thoughts. I was very impulsive and they were out of control. An example would be: if my side hurt . . . I'd find myself way down the road, in my imagination, at MY FUNERAL! That's how out of control I was. I was afraid all of the time and had no hope for a future.

I didn't trust God because I didn't know him. I didn't know Him because I believed lies about Him.

It took time and patience on His part and mine, too. But with time and lots of love, I can honestly say that He loves me. His heart is good. I don't have God figured out. I am never going to be able to do that. He's God! But He is my Father and He has a plan for my life, for me, to prosper me . . . not to harm me.

I love the definition of hope. If you do an internet search, you will find synonyms like this… it breaks Hope down for us. It's big! And I love words because of this! Look how it's broken down:

aspiration
desire
wish
expectation
ambition
aim
plan
dream
daydream
pipe dream
longing
yearning
craving
hankering

And the list goes on. It's almost like, if you can think of anything good and amazing, you can just add it to the list.

I hope so. I hope he loves me. I hope I get the weekend off. I hope that they come for a visit. I hope she is pregnant. I hope he isn't mad at me.

What are you hoping for?

I want you to stay there. I want you to resist the negative at all costs. I want you to pay attention to how things are making you feel. I hope that you will take control of what you allow to rent space in your head.

If you are scrolling on FB and suddenly your heart starts racing, your breathing speeds up, you become jealous and critical. Stop. If you catch your thinking racing away from you . . . say this out loud and strong: "NEXT!!!"

Everytime you catch your thoughts running away, you can stop them.

Activation

Pay attention to what you are feeling. Consider what is robbing you. Get tuned in to where your thoughts are. Take control of your thought life. I like to declare, "NEXT". It works.

And when you shock your thinking, choose to think about things that are authentic and real, honorable, admirable, beautiful, respectful, pure, holy, merciful and kind. Set your thoughts on the glorious work of God, praising Him always.

Scriptures for you to ponder and apply:

Philippians 4:8, Hebrews 6:19, Romans 5:5, Hebrews 11:1.

Prayer:

Jesus - Thank you for giving me all that I need to build my trust in you. Please help me to embrace your word and teach me how to apply it to my life and my thinking. I ask you to be the Lord of my thoughts, the Lord of my emotions. I want to trust you. I want to see more of you. Thank you for your mercy and your kindness in my life.

Chapter 34

Let Jesus Lead You

I think the most important thing to me - when it really comes down to it - is knowing that Jesus is in it with me.

And He is. Thank God!

I cannot get around in this life without Him.

Aaron and I teach our girls from that place—this raw, real place of dependence.

We need Him. Every day. Every breath.

And I want to bring something home to you today.

When we're hurting…
When we are falling apart…
When we are grieving, confused, lonely, or overwhelmed…
We are vulnerable.
We are prone to deception.

It's in these tender, cracked-open moments that the enemy likes to whisper things that sound spiritual but carry no truth.

It's in those low places that we might start grabbing onto anything that sounds like hope—but if we're not grounded in the Word, we'll end up clinging to counterfeits.

We will not always agree with everyone.
We're just not going to.
Not here. Not on this side of heaven.

That's why we have to know the Word for ourselves.
We have to filter everything—every podcast, every post, every prophecy, every conversation—through the Holy Spirit. Literally everything!

Because if we don't know the Truth, we will get pulled along from hither to thither, from one emotional high to the next spiritual-sounding opinion.

And eventually, if we're not anchored…
We'll believe anything.

Truth isn't something we visit once a week.
Truth is a person.
Truth is Jesus.

Activation

Take 10 quiet minutes and ask the Holy Spirit:

Have I been receiving anything lately that didn't come from You?

Is there something I've taken to heart that I need to release?

Am I speaking from a healed place—or from a place that still needs healing?

How can I stay grounded in Your truth this week?

Then open your Bible.

Read one chapter. Out loud. Slowly. Listen to yourself while you read. Faith comes by hearing.

Let His truth become your anchor again.

Prayer

Jesus,
Thank You for being all in with me.
I need You—I cannot do this life without You.

Help me to hear Your voice above all the noise.
Teach me to filter what I receive and what I speak through Your Spirit.
I only want what is true, what is pure, what is You.

Make me a person of Truth, anchored in the Word and led by the Spirit.
In my weakness, You are strong. In all of it, You are faithful.

I trust You. Amen.

Chapter 35

Suddenly

My God! My God . . . Why is it so hard to trust You in this one place?

I want to. I want to trust you. I want to.

Sometimes these are the only words that I can muster up. I really want to.

I want to crawl up in Your lap and just be held. I just want You.

Some days I just feel the questions well up in my soul. Why? What? Who? How? When? Where?

Some days I just whisper, "help."

Sometimes I can't say anything. Some days I can't feel anything except for the heaviness in my soul. Other days I only feel pain creeping into my flesh.

I want to throw it all at You. I want to "let You". I want to crawl up onto Your lap but . . . .

Have you ever had days like this? They sometimes seem to last forever. And then suddenly, there we are, together, dancing.

Suddenly, we are dancing in the rain. Suddenly, all we can feel is the sun on our skin. Suddenly, a kiss on our forehead from someone who loves us deeply. Suddenly, an embrace that melts it all away.

Suddenly . . . .

It's the sudden suddenlies in our lives that heal the painful moments that we thought would last forever. And then, suddenly, we smile again.

I can still feel the heaviness in my soul. I can still feel how that heaviness affects my body but suddenly it's not as big as it was.

He is our wonderful God of suddenlies. He loves. He sees. He hears. He is alive and well and calls for us every moment of every day to join Him in life. Life! Alive! I am alive!

Suddenly, I am alive!

Childhood abuse wreaks havoc on us and devastates our souls. We learned not to trust. We learned that there is probably something wrong with us because something bad kept happening to us. We learned very early on that we must be bad. We learn very early on that people aren't safe. We learn that maybe our body is our enemy just because it continues to betray me.

The ultimate betrayal…

My body let me down. Because of my body, bad things happened. And no one protected me from the bad things that happened and so therefore I must be bad.

Is that how you feel when something seems to go wrong in your body as an adult? It is a very lonely and isolating struggle. I get it!

The struggle is real and today I am there. I am waiting for a "suddenly."

I want to encourage you with something. I am in this with you. Let's look for the 'suddenlies', together, today. Right now!

I want to share with you the first 3 suddenlies that happened to me while writing this chapter.

1. The Father's Song - Upperroom

2. A kiss on the forehead from my husband

3. YOU!

When I remember that I am loved and that I am not alone, really… I find great comfort.

I want that to happen for you today. Let's do this together. Let's slow down a little bit and quieten our world just a little bit.

What does that look like for you? You are in control of this moment. You are in control of the very atmosphere around you. Let's try this activation together.

Activation

Take a deep breath in and close your eyes. I am doing this with you. Don't forget to breathe out.

Listen to the sounds around you. What do you hear? Does it make you anxious? Does it give you peace? If it makes you anxious . . . move. I'll wait.

Are you ready to move on?

What do you smell? Is it clean? Is it lovely? Breathe deeply. Breathe in slowly and exhale. As you exhale, let go.

Release the stress. Breathe in and out until you feel the release.

How do you feel?

Where are your thoughts? Are you afraid? Are you fixated on something that you feel in your body? Do you have pain? Do you feel pain in a certain area of your body? If you do not - great! Don't create something, just move on. But if you feel something in your body let's do this together. Put your hand where it hurts and speak to the pain.

Do this with me: "God is bigger than pain." Say that. Speak the Blood of Jesus over that pain.

Breathe in YAH and breathe out WEH. YAHWEH is your breath! This is not about making any pain go away. There is no magic formula for that. I mean there might be but that's witchcraft!

We want to practice shifting our thoughts.

Keep your thoughts continually fixed on all that is authentic and real, honorable and admirable, beautiful and respectful, pure and holy, merciful and kind. And fasten your thoughts on every glorious work of God, praising him always. (Philippians 4:8 TPT)

I'm struggling! Ok. Let's do this again.

YAH - WEH! Give Him all that hurts. Inside and out. Let it go. Weep if you want. Let the dam break, Let go.

Close your eyes and listen. I hear Him saying: "I love you. I love you. I love you. I love you. I love you. Come close. Let me pour my love on you. Let me love you. I'll protect you. I'll defend you. You can trust me. I am good. I will never leave you. Rest in me."

Let's leave this right here.

Please practice this activation daily. Get alone. Breathe in. Breathe out. Say His name as you breathe in and out. Think about what is good and pure. Practice elevating your thoughts.

Sing this song over yourself: Jesus loves me, this I know. Sing it until you believe it. And then keep singing it.

Talk to Abba. And then listen. Tell Him how you feel and then listen.

That's your assignment.

Beloved. You are loved. I am loved. We are valuable. We are His prize, His legacy. He can't abandon us, He won't. He desires you, me, us. Take His grace today and breathe.

I love you. He loves you. I am praying for you today to receive all that He has for you.

and suddenly . . . .

Chapter 36

Using the Crap From Your Past

Lately, I have been in a place of deep grief and regret. I'm just going to be honest with you. Can we please just get real? In my experience, it's the only way to heal.

It's not that I haven't wanted to talk about it, but my feelings sometimes seem so repetitive and embarrassing. I often stuff them down and down and down until . . . they start coming up. And then without me knowing what's going on, I'm grumpy and stale and sad and "blah, blah" . . .

When I do feel like I need a good cry, that's all I think I need and so I just keep going.

But God help the person who is sitting with me when that emotional lump that's been stuck in my throat pops and I ugly weep! It's always my husband because I haven't found anyone else that I trust that much.

Last night, I was in pain. The kind of pain that feels like it's just always there. The pain of grief. The pain of regret. The pain of loss and loneliness. The pain of shame and the feelings of diminishment. The ache of truth of what actually happened to us as children. But, I am convinced that when we are abused as children over and over, something happens that stays with us all of our lives.

It's messed up in many ways!

I was "fine" until I entered into my 50's and realized all the potential and dreams that are inside of me. Last night I told my husband that I think I would have been a totally different person if it hadn't been for the neglect and betrayal of people who should have protected me.

OK, I wasn't fine, but I had more energy and juice to run myself into the ground so that I either felt nothing or I was too busy to notice what was there.

I have walked through years of healing for the trauma in my soul. I have walked through forgiveness and even have walked through the grief of "letting go" of what I actually never had with some of my family of origin.

And then internalizing the pros and cons of writing a book, how to honor, how to be honest, how to help people, how to ...... on and on until I just quit.

I put this book down for a while. I told God and my husband that I am not going to finish the book. I decided that I'm done and it's pointless. The frustration in all of that is so intense and confusing!

At the time I am writing this chapter, I work in a behavioral health clinic with a lot of people who have a lot of letters behind their names. Sometimes, they like to talk about that. It's a trigger for me because it just feels so diminishing. It isn't their fault. It just is a reminder to me that I feel like a failure and I just didn't have a choice to do what I think I would have been great at doing.

Yesterday was that 'straw that broke the camel's back' for me at work. It was too much and I felt like I was literally the bottom of my shoe that just stepped in dog crap.

But it isn't just that.

It's the change in my body, entering into the middle aged season of life and menopause right around the corner. All of the stuff that comes with being a woman turning 52.

Last night, Aaron and I were walking through a fun activation with our 2 youngest girls. It was pretty encouraging but challenging for one of my kids and maybe, if I am honest, challenging for all of us.

The question was to name 5 things that we love about ourselves.

Later, when Aaron and I decided to hang out in our suite, it all came out. Little by little, I began to process my soul hurts. I had no idea what was happening until I felt that painful lump in my throat. I just let it come and I allowed myself to feel all of it.

As I processed, Aaron listened.

He walked away just for a minute, turned around and said, "use the crap from your past to fertilize your future". And then he reminded me of all that I have overcome and all that I have done and all of the ones that I have loved. He reminded me of the life that I have made, with him and with Jesus.

I needed every single word that came out of that man's mouth! It was salve for my soul. I felt clean and new and fresh. And so, I picked up the pen again today to carry on with laboring through the pages of this book.

The Way Out . . . use the crap from your past to fertilize your future.

I have been secretly sitting in shame because I have been comparing who I think I could have been to who I see myself as. I could have been a detective, and a forensic detective at that! Or a chef, a scientist, a horticulturist or botanist!

But instead . . . because I was born and raised in an environment where I was not protected from abuse, I instantly became orphaned . . .

...all of the thoughts, emotions, and regret that can come as a result of reflecting on the injustice of the bad choices I did not make, but were made upon me...

But now...

I am . . . a loving mother, a passionate lover of beauty. I am the treasured wife to my beloved husband who is my best friend and lover. A daughter of the King, an empathetic friend.

So, I have, unknowingly, taken crap from my past to fertilize my future and I would not trade it for anything.

I am familiar with suffering and so I can understand and relate to suffering. I relate to the worst of the worst that you have been through. And I have the authority to speak into it because I have overcome such deep, deep pain and trauma.

Jesus is with us.

He is not afraid to walk though our dark nights with us. He wants to. Holy Spirit is the greatest comfort to us when we are hurting and feel like no one can possibly understand us. Maybe people can't and don't but there is One. And He gave us a good Dad - One who cheers for us and loves us and knows us and is passionate about us. He's not mad at you. He has wonderful things ahead, just for you!

Activation

Just be kind to you. Tell yourself that you love YOU. You need to look yourself in the eyes and love who you are in there!

Go and tell yourself 5 things that you love about you. Ask those close to you to do that same and then you do that for them.

I love _______ about me!

I love _______ about me!

I love _______ about me!

I love _______ about me!

I love _______ about me!

Prayer:

Jesus,

You see the whole story.

The moments that crushed me.

The people who betrayed me.

The tears I cried when no one was watching.

You never looked away. Not once.

There were times I thought my pain disqualified me,

that I was too broken, too messy, too far gone.

But I'm starting to see—You never saw me that way.

Even when I didn't feel it, You were gathering the pieces.

Not to throw them away…

But to redeem them.

Thank You for using what the enemy meant to destroy me to deepen me instead.

Thank You that my suffering has made me tender,

that I can feel with others and not just for them.

That I've learned to love from the same place where I once bled.

Nothing is wasted—not the silence, not the sorrow, not the scars.

You are the God who turns graves into gardens,

ashes into beauty,

and wounds into testimonies.

So today, I give You what's left in my hands—

even if it's trembling, even if it's small.

Make it holy, God.

Make it matter.

And as You do, remind me that I'm not behind.

I'm becoming.

In Jesus' name,

Amen.

Chapter 37

Declarations & Proclamations

Declaring the Word of the Lord over your life is powerful and necessary for growth and healing. This is something that I have practiced over the years and have even witnessed self-deliverance.

Fill your soul with God's Word. Eat it, drink it, speak it.

We are no longer orphans but Daughters of the Most High!

As God continues to restore me to my rightful place in Him, delivering me from what is left of an orphan-minded girl . . . He told me to stand and declare these things.

I want to share these with you because they have been downloaded into me from Abba. We are no longer orphans but Daughters. We are not abandoned but connected. We are called to sit (in the heavenlies), walk (in the Spirit), and stand (in the armor).

Feel free to share, declare and proclaim as often as possible until you no longer need to look at these printed declarations. Everything that Jesus owns is ours.

Everything.

We are co-heirs. We have a generous Abba who has seated us in the heavenlies, in the high places. We WILL do greater things than Jesus!

1. He has healed me and so I will help to heal others.
2. He has given freely to me and so I will freely give to others.
3. He has loved me with abandon and so I will love others with abandon.
4. He has restored me and so I will restore others.
5. He has forgiven me and so I will forgive others.
6. He has redeemed me and so I will help redeem others.
7. He has walked with me and so I will walk with others.
8. He is a friend to me and so I will be a friend to others.
9. He has comforted me and so I will comfort others.

10. He has lifted me out of the pit and so I will lift others.
11. He has encouraged me and so I will encourage others.

Feel free to add to this as you remember all that God has done for you! Freely give what you have been given.

Declarations with Scripture References:

1. He has healed me and so I will help to heal others
— Isaiah 53:5; Matthew 10:8

2. He has given freely to me and so I will freely give to others
— Matthew 10:8; 2 Corinthians 9:7

3. He has loved me with abandon and so I will love others with abandon
— 1 John 4:19; John 13:34-35

4. He has restored me and so I will restore others
— Psalm 23:3; Galatians 6:1

5. He has forgiven me and so I will forgive others
— Ephesians 4:32; Colossians 3:13

6. He has redeemed me and so I will help redeem others
— Ephesians 1:7; Jude 1:23

7. He has walked with me and so I will walk with others
— Isaiah 43:2; Galatians 6:2

8. He is a friend to me and so I will be a friend to others
— John 15:15; Proverbs 17:17

9. He has comforted me and so I will comfort others
— 2 Corinthians 1:3-4

10. He has lifted me out of the pit and so I will lift others
— Psalm 40:2; Isaiah 58:6-7

11. He has encouraged me and so I will encourage other
— 2 Thessalonians 2:16-17; 1 Thessalonians 5:11

Chapter 38

Be My Valentine

"Call my name and forever you will be mine. My heart is a safe place. You are on the edge of something beautiful, won't you just let go?" - Jesus

You are worthy. You were then and you are now.

Were you ever told as a child that you weren't worthy? Were you rejected as a child? Were you betrayed or neglected? It wasn't because you weren't worthy. It wasn't because you weren't worth love and attention. It was because of what was on the inside of them. It was because of their hearts and because of their lack.

Beloved. You. Are. Worthy. You are worth the life that Jesus chose to give. You are worth the blood that Jesus chose to spill. You were worth it then and you are worth it now.

Who told you that you weren't worth it? Who told you that you don't have worth? Did Jesus tell you that right after He knocked on the door of your heart? Did He say . . . . "I love you and that's why I am saving you. You aren't worthy of my blood being spilled and you are not worthy of Me laying my body down, but I'll do it anyway."

Friend, religion told you that. False humility told you that you aren't worthy. Deserving and being worthy are two different things. Because of Jesus we don't get what we deserve. Hallelujah!

I was in a conversation with Holy Spirit today that was more like a dance. It was so sweet and pure and good. He danced and danced through my heart with words of Truth. He spoke to me with pictures and words and visions. I want to let you in on that for a minute. While it was so precious, it broke my heart.

He asked me, "what parent would ever tell their little boy or girl that they aren't worth the gift that is brought to them while still bringing the gift".

He showed me children who have been broken to pieces by those who should have loved them. He showed me little children who were told how unworthy they are of love and gifts and safety and hugs. Those little children grew up in low self esteem and with worthless fruits.

And, at some point these children grew up and had a head on collision with Jesus. They are now born again and are attending church and meeting other Christians. And then they hear . . . . we are not worthy, I am not worthy, you are not worthy BUT God, in spite of you, loves you because of who He is. It's not about you Christian, at all. It's really all about God and His love for you.

While that is true in a way… Christian is now hearing the same thing that he heard from his abusers as a child. Christian can't understand the difference between his earthly parents and the God who saved him and loves Him enough to sacrifice His only beloved Son.

We really need to stop saying these things. While these words may not carry weight with you, it really is heavy for some. It was for me.

I am thankful that Abba has shown me that His heart is a safe place and that He loves me. He loves me because He loves me but He saved me because He thought I was worth it! He saw my worth before the foundation of the earth was laid out! He made me in His image. I am His image bearer. I am a daughter of the King! I am worthy because He made me. Don't be afraid to say that over yourself. I am worthy of His blood! I am worthy of His body being laid down.

God named me. God got personal with me when He first dreamt about me. God got personal with me when His Son said . . . I'll go! Jesus said I will go!

Don't be afraid to accept your worth and value. That doesn't make you arrogant or proud. It aligns your spirit with His Spirit and the truth about who you are.

Meditate on PSALMS 139: 1-18 (TPT)…

"You Know All About Me
Lord, you know everything there is to know about me.
You perceive every movement of my heart and soul,
and you understand my every thought before it even enters my mind.
You are so intimately aware of me, Lord.
You read my heart like an open book
and you know all the words I'm about to speak
before I even start a sentence!
You know every step I will take before my journey even begins.
You've gone into my future to prepare the way,
and in kindness you follow behind me

to spare me from the harm of my past.
You have laid your hand on me!
This is just too wonderful, deep, and incomprehensible!
Your understanding of me brings me wonder and strength.
Where could I go from your Spirit?
Where could I run and hide from your face?
If I go up to heaven, you're there!
If I go down to the realm of the dead, you're there too!
If I fly with wings into the shining dawn, you're there!
If I fly into the radiant sunset, you're there waiting!
Wherever I go, your hand will guide me;
Your strength will empower me.``
It's impossible to disappear from you
or to ask the darkness to hide me,
for your presence is everywhere, bringing light into my night.
There is no such thing as darkness with you.
The night, to you, is as bright as the day;
there's no difference between the two.
You formed my innermost being, shaping my delicate inside
and my intricate outside,
and wove them all together in my mother's womb.
I thank you, God, for making me so mysteriously complex!
Everything you do is marvelously breathtaking.
It simply amazes me to think about it!
How thoroughly you know me, Lord!
You even formed every bone in my body
when you created me in the secret place;
carefully, skillfully you shaped me from nothing to something.
You saw who you created me to be before I became me!
Before I'd ever seen the light of day,
the number of days you planned for me
were already recorded in your book.
Every single moment you are thinking of me!
How precious and wonderful to consider
that you cherish me constantly in your every thought!
O God, your desires toward me are more
than the grains of sand on every shore!
When I awake each morning, you're still with me."

I want to encourage you with this activation. Ready?

Hold out your hands. Give Abba every lie that you have ever believed about Him. Ask Him to help you recall those lies. Wait. Confess that to Him. Ask Him what the truth is. Ask Him to speak that truth over your precious Heart. Receive it. Speak that over yourself over and over and over until you finally believe it. You will begin to hold your head up before you know it in that area where you have believed a lie about Him. And now . . . ask God where you have believed a lie about your own self. Reject the lies, turn to Abba and let Him wash you with His love. You are worthy.

I know that you are worthy because Jesus gave you everything that belongs to Him. It's amazing when we step into that truth! It will change everything.

The next time you hear someone say that they are not worthy . . . pray for them because they are trapped in performance and religion.

Benediction

The Way Out

A Benediction for the Brave

You made it.

You showed up. You read through pages that touched deep wounds. You lingered in places that many avoid. And you didn't just survive this journey - you began to heal.

Maybe you're not all the way out yet. That's okay. Healing isn't a doorway you rush through - it's a path you walk with Jesus. Day by day. Layer by layer. Moment by sacred moment.

But here's what I want you to know:

There is a way out.

Out of shame.
Out of silence.
Out of pretending.
Out of surviving.

Jesus is the Way.

And He doesn't just pull you from the wreckage—He walks with you until you are walking on water. Until the nightmares lose their grip. Until the mirror stops lying. Until your story becomes your strength. Until you look around and realize: You're not the same anymore.

You are loved.
You are not alone.
And you are worth the work.

Let every page you've just walked through become a door—opening wide into freedom, into truth, into rest, into joy.

Let every scar become a sentence in your testimony.
Let every valley become a garden.

He's not just healing you.
He's sending you.
Because now… you carry the map.
You carry the mercy.

And when someone you love says,
"I don't know how to get out of this," you'll look them in the eye, with strength in your voice and compassion in your bones, and you'll say:

"I do. Let me show you the way out."

About the Author

Jennifer Schulman is a wife, mother, prophetic voice, and healing guide whose life and message are rooted in restoration, courage, and the tender nearness of Jesus. Her journey through deep personal trauma and decades of healing has equipped her to lead others into wholeness with honesty, grace, and Spirit-led insight.

Jennifer has been happily married to her husband, Aaron, for over twenty years. Together, they have raised three wonderful daughters who are her greatest joy and legacy. Their home in Central Ohio is full of life—with laughter, healing conversations around the table, and the occasional fur tumble from their beloved Bernese Mountain Dogs.

Jennifer finds joy in the simple and sacred: cooking meals for those she loves, cultivating flowers and indoor plants, capturing beauty through photography, and encouraging her family and friends with words that build up and breathe life.

Whether through writing, speaking, or prophetic ministry, Jennifer's heart is to create safe spaces where people feel seen, known, and invited into deeper intimacy with God. Her story is a living testimony that freedom is possible, healing is real, and love always makes a way out.

To learn more or connect with Jennifer, visit https://www.wayoutbook.com

JOIN US & BECOME A VIP

You're not alone… and your journey is just beginning.

You picked up "The Way Out" for a reason.
Maybe you're confronting deep wounds.
Maybe you're supporting someone you love.
Maybe you're simply hoping someone understands.

We do. And we're offering to walk with you…

Take the Next Step — Walk Deeper with Us

Introducing the "Way Out AudioBook & Intimate Conversations"
More than just audio... it's healing, raw, and real.

Jennifer reads each chapter aloud, then she and Aaron share unfiltered, heart-level conversations about every topic - offering insights from 21+ years of healing in marriage, trauma recovery, and life with Jesus.

Real Stories. Real Healing. Real Breakthrough.
* Listen while driving, walking, or with your small group
* Perfect for journaling or deep discussions
* Hours of honest, Spirit-led audio you'll return to for life

FREE VIP ACCESS - Just for Readers - Get exclusive content when you join:
* FREE sample of our Audio + Conversation Series
* First access to new workshops & livestreams
* VIP-only videos, teachings & healing tools
* Bonus activations & behind-the-scenes insights

SCAN THIS QR CODE NOW - to unlock your free material and one-time offer - Only available to readers like you or visit: www.wayoutbook.com/VIP

Your journey toward healing doesn't end with a book. It begins with a relationship - With God… with yourself… and with a community that's walked the road too… We'll walk it with you.

— Jennifer & Aaron Schulman

www.ingramcontent.com/pod-product-compliance
Lightning Source LLC
LaVergne TN
LVHW012332100826
845148LV00017B/2116